THE ART OF COLOURFUL STITCHING

EXPRESSIVE EMBROIDERY

Chloë Amy Avery

THE ART OF COLOURFUL STITCHING

EXPRESSIVE EMBROIDERY

THE CROWOOD PRESS

CONTENTS

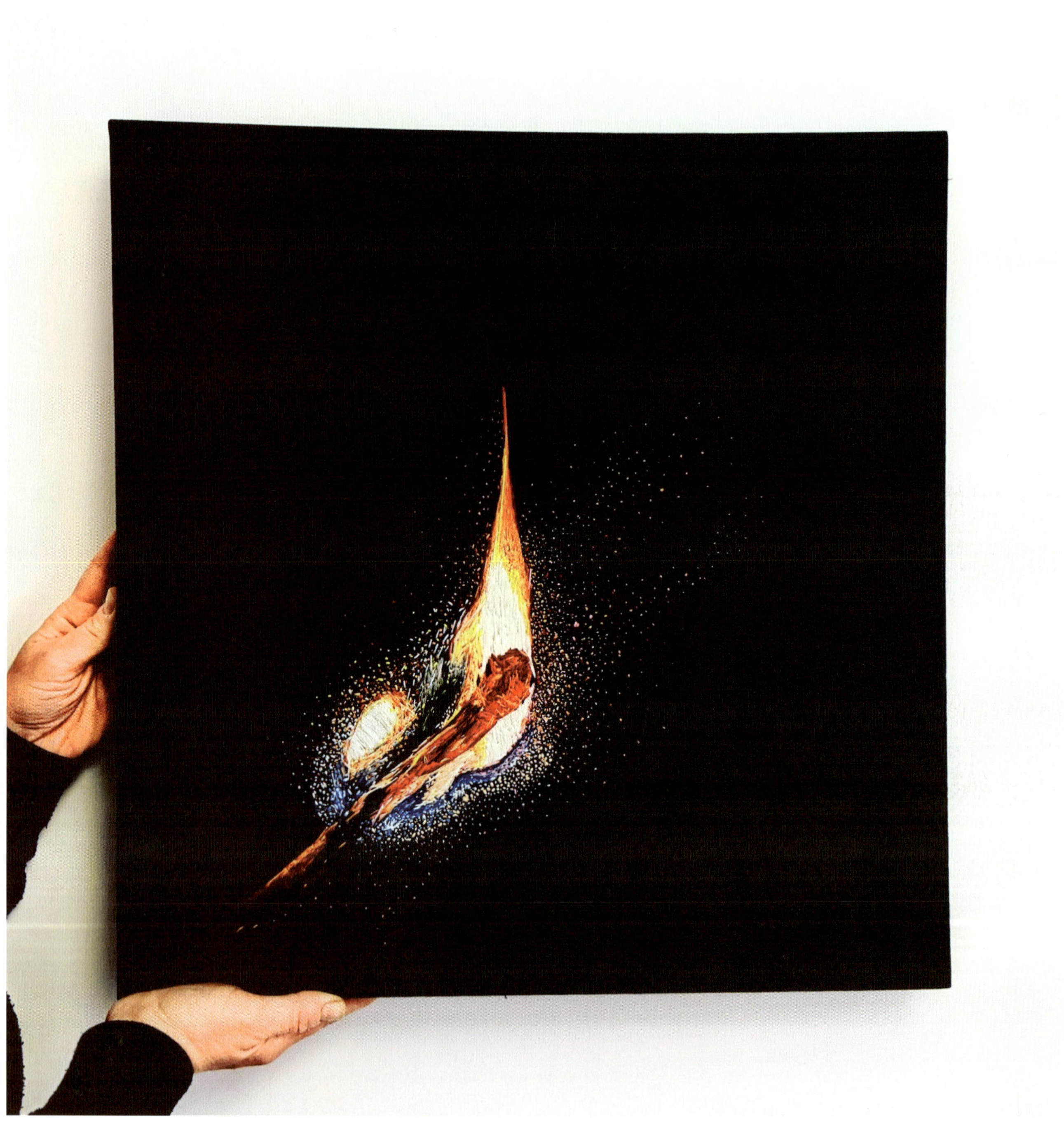

INTRODUCTION

In every corner of the world, from the bustling streets of New York to the serene villages of Peru, the art of embroidery weaves together the threads of tradition, culture and heritage. Passed down from generation to generation, this timeless craft is more than just a form of decorative needlework; it is a testament to the resilience of human creativity and the continued bonds between families and communities.

Embroidery has deep roots in history, with evidence of its practice dating back thousands of years. From the elaborate designs adorning ancient Egyptian garments to the intricate patterns and figures stitched into medieval tapestries, embroidery has been used to embellish textiles and tell stories for centuries. As civilisations flourished and traded with one another, embroidery techniques travelled across the world, evolving and adapting to reflect the unique traditions of each region.

A STITCHED CULTURE

In many civilisations, embroidery serves as a vibrant tapestry, reflecting the values, beliefs and aesthetics of its people. In India, the colourful threads of traditional embroidery such as kantha and chikankari mirror the rich tapestry of Indian life, with motifs inspired by nature, mythology and daily rituals. In China, the delicate art of silk embroidery has been revered for its intricacy and beauty for over 2,000 years, with many embroidered motifs symbolising prosperity, longevity and happiness.

The vibrant hues of traditional Mexican embroidery, such as Otomi and Tenango, celebrate the country's indigenous heritage. Its motifs are inspired by ancient Mesoamerican art and folklore. As a contrast, the crisp simplicity of Nordic embroidery reflects the region's stark landscapes and strong sense of community, with its designs often featuring geometric patterns and inspiration drawn from nature.

Polish Kashubian embroidery is a stunning representation of culture and folklore, with an emphasis on colour. There are only seven colours used, each representing an aspect of the abundance of the land.

Across the world embroidery is an expression of cultural society; it is a rich source for the conversations and communities that are built around the craft of hand stitching.

From Generation to Generation

Across cultures, the tradition of embroidery is lovingly passed down from one generation to the next, forging bonds that transcend time and distance. In many families, mothers teach their daughters the art of embroidery as a rite of passage, imparting not only practical skills but also the stories, memories and traditions woven into each stitch.

Grandmothers stitch alongside granddaughters, sharing tales of their own youth. In community centres and cultural institutions, elder artisans pass on their knowledge, ensuring that the traditions of embroidery continue to stay alive. Embroidery has brought people together for generations.

Stitching the Future

As the world evolves and cultures intermingle, embroidery remains a vital thread connecting past, present and future. In an era of mass production and digitalisation, the handmade beauty of embroidered textiles holds a special allure, reminding us of history and the stories embedded in every thread.

As new generations embrace the art of embroidery, they bring their own perspectives, techniques and innovations to this ancient craft, ensuring its relevance for years to come. The changes in our recent cost of living and awareness of our planet's vulnerability caused by consumption has led to embroidery becoming even more attractive as people embrace a less disposable culture, utilising upcycling as a way of playing a part in caring for our planet and thinking of generations to come. Whether preserving traditional motifs or pushing the boundaries of design, embroiderers around the world continue to stitch together the fabric of our shared humanity, one delicate thread at a time.

This book has been created for you to learn the basics of embroidery, learn how to create your own pieces inspired by things you love and learn to develop your own style. It adds a contemporary edge to embroidery, bringing it up to date and helping you create pieces that you are excited to stitch and share. Each chapter will help to explore ways to create embroideries that are more than stitch-by-numbers; you will learn how to engage with design and develop your own ideas. The journey of how to explore creativity from the process of inspiration through to producing finished embroidered pieces will enrich your embroidery experience, giving you the knowledge you need to develop your own style and the skills to refine and edit your ideas for the best results.

Once you're confident in the basics of embroidery, stitches, tools and colour selection, you will be able to experiment with a better understanding, building on the foundations and creating freely.

Before we start, I will explain a little about myself. As a child I would spend hours creating, drawing and trying to sew under the watchful eye of my mother, who owned a sewing machine and taught me all she could about using it and being creative with fabric and crafts. I grew up in a television-free home so creativity was encouraged and 'I'm bored' was banned. Maybe it was out of those times of feeling at a loss to know how to entertain myself that I learnt to explore and experiment with my creativity. If drawing was involved, I would enter competitions and spend hours on school projects. I found reading and writing challenging and later – much later – discovered I was dyslexic, which explained my years of frustration and struggle with academia. I did, however, try very hard despite my restraints and I believe it has made me a hard worker and determined to push boundaries. At 16, I left school to study fashion design, as it was one of the few courses I could do at that age which allowed me to spend 80 per cent of my time being creative. I loved it. I adored the variety of designing, sewing and painting in life drawing classes. The opportunity to spend all day using my hands and creating from my imagination was wonderful and released me from the struggle I had experienced with my reading and writing.

It was during my studies in my fashion design and surface textiles degree that I was diagnosed with dyslexia, which although it hadn't held me back, helped me understand why I had found some things more challenging up until that point. I went on to study surface textile for fashion to MA level, but by the end the last thing I wanted to do was get a job in the industry. However, it gave me my love of everything colour, texture and textiles. It was only a short while after finishing my MA that I had my first child. I always wanted my children to be a priority, which meant I became self-employed so I could work around my family. I made bespoke patterns and clothes for a while but it didn't quite fulfil my desperate need for creativity. As a family we moved abroad for a few years and this is where my love for embroidery came into play. I missed home and found the language challenging. I had some knowledge of embroidery and I needed to create in order to escape and process the things I missed and loved about London – the city both me and my husband grew up in.

As I started longing for things that were not available, I had the urge to document this in a way that I felt honoured my memories and my culture. To be honest, I have fond memories of this time. It was tough in many ways but sometimes the best things come out of adversity. I wanted to pull together my love of drawing, painting, colour and texture – what better way to do this than start embroidering? I had the basics down from my childhood and the techniques I had learnt during my degree. When I picked up a needle and thread and started to use them in a way that made me happy, it started to look like paint on a canvas so I thought I would challenge myself to create almost realistic images using simple stitch techniques. I embroidered in a way that was comfortable and felt natural to me.

It's taken me years of embroidery to find my signature style but still my inspiration tends to stem from its starting point; culture and nostalgia. Whether it's food that identifies and brings people together or a bunch of flowers symbolic of sympathy and love, these are the things that still inspire me to paint with thread. This book will take you on an embroidery journey, so you can discover what you love and how to create productively. Throughout the book you will be taken through the processes involved in embroidery, how to create your own designs and how to produce a collection and present it.

The book is divided into chapters that will go into details about the process of embroidery. As a part of the process, you will be given a step-by-step guide to each project. This of course is a guideline for your creative process; this is all my knowledge and experience for you to learn from and run with in your own way. It will give you the scaffolding you need to excel as an embroiderer. Take the ideas and the basic structure and make them your own. The ideas will give you a chance to experiment and grow for each process. There are different levels within each chapter, so as you progress you can take on the next challenge with growing confidence.

I believe embroidery is a fun and exciting way to be creative; age and experience need not be a barrier. My hope is that my book will show you that embroidery doesn't have to be perfect and can be completely individual. As you learn, it should be an expression of yourself. Take my ideas and suggestions and experiment with them, so you flourish in your own creativity. Remember there are no mistakes; if you are not overly satisfied with your embroidery or a project, learn from the experience and let that drive you through to your next project. Above all, embroidery should be enjoyable and relaxing.

T
TROPICAL
Mine

CHAPTER 1

FULLY EQUIPPED

Embroidery, from experience, has been a way of expressing creativity, but also a huge help to my mental health. Any amount of experience can give you a chance to explore your creativity. Concentrating when keeping your hands and brain engaged in a task can give your mind an escape from reality. Whether you pick up a needle and thread for a few minutes or for hours at a time, either is a great tool for expressing yourself. You may find that your work reflects the season you're in, or it may be a way of communicating feelings that words can't articulate. For some, embroidery may be a pastime, something that you can dip in and out of, for others it may be an essential to fulfil their need for creativity or just to switch off. You may be at the start of a new business idea using embroidery, or an artist like myself. This chapter is here to help you organise your tools and work out what to use and how to use it, to make your embroidery journey the most pleasant experience possible.

This chapter will give you tips and suggestions from my years of experience to help you focus as you start out or progress. I have been asked so many questions about what to use, how to go about sourcing and finding tools that work for all sorts of scenarios. This chapter should give you a rich knowledge from my expertise so you can run with your ideas and produce beautiful embroideries, no matter what your style.

The first bit of advice is to try it – don't get stuck with something and keep persevering if it has taken the joy out of embroidery. You must experiment with fabric, thread, needles, scissors, hoops and even storage. You need to find how you like to work.

Before you get started, ask yourself a few questions. Who are you stitching for? Is it for yourself, a hobby? Are you producing embroidered gifts? Are you starting an embroidery business? Are you a textiles student?

So, where do we begin?

FABRIC

The questions I am asked most frequently are about fabric and what to choose. Ask yourself what the fabric is for. If you can get a needle through it, you can stitch on it. You could make holes in wood or metal and still stitch through it, if that is a look you're going for.

Embroidery, an art form dating back centuries, finds its perfect partner in cotton fabric. Known for its versatility, durability and softness, cotton provides a superb canvas for intricate stitching and vibrant designs. Let's delve into the benefits of using cotton fabric for embroidery and explore the various types of cottons available for your creative endeavours.

Woven fabrics are great to embroider on; the key is that if they are woven rather than knitted, the fabric is less likely to have stretch. Cotton is a popular choice for embroidery, as the less movement when the fabric is under tension the better. Brushed cotton, linen, calico, poplin, canvas, muslin, drill, twill, denim, gingham and lawn are all excellent cottons to stitch on, with great structure. Cotton is a reliable fabric when creating embroideries to hang on walls, and its versatility makes creating clothes in these fabric types easy, which then makes the process of embroidery onto a garment much more straightforward.

Gingham cotton.

Coloured cottons.

The Benefits of Cotton Fabric for Embroidery

- Softness: Cotton's natural softness makes it comfortable to work with, allowing needles to glide smoothly through the fabric. This ensures that your embroidery stitches are precise and even, resulting in a professional finish.
- Breathability: Cotton fabric is highly breathable, allowing air to circulate freely. This characteristic prevents moisture build-up, making cotton ideal for embroidery projects that require long hours of stitching.
- Absorbency: Cotton fibres have excellent absorbent properties, making them perfect for taking up dyes and retaining vibrant colours. This ensures that your embroidered designs remain vivid and true to their original hues over time.
- Durability: Cotton is renowned for its durability and strength, ensuring that your embroidered creations withstand the test of time. Whether you're crafting heirloom pieces or everyday wear, cotton fabric provides longevity and resilience.
- Versatility: From delicate handkerchiefs to sturdy denim jackets, cotton fabric can be found in a wide range of weights and weaves, making it suitable for various embroidery techniques and applications.

Different Types of Cottons for Embroidery

- Cotton broadcloth: This lightweight, plain-weave fabric is commonly used for embroidery projects such as linens, quilts and clothing. Its smooth surface allows for intricate stitching, while its affordability makes it accessible to beginners and seasoned embroiderers alike.
- Cotton twill: Twill-weave cotton fabric, characterised by its diagonal rib pattern, offers excellent stability and drape making it suitable for embroidery projects that require structure and flexibility. It is often used for embellishing garments, accessories and home decor items.
- Cotton voile: Known for its sheer, airy quality, cotton voile is a favourite among embroiderers for creating delicate, ethereal designs. Its soft, lightweight nature lends itself well to projects such as curtains, scarves and bridal wear, where a touch of elegance is desired.
- Cotton denim: Renowned for its rugged durability and distinctive texture, cotton denim provides a unique canvas for embroidery projects with a casual, rustic aesthetic. From embellished jeans to embroidered jackets, denim offers endless possibilities for creative expression.
- Organic cotton: For eco-conscious embroiderers, organic cotton is a sustainable choice that prioritises environmental and social responsibility. Grown without synthetic pesticides or fertilisers, organic cotton is gentle on the earth and produces fibres of exceptional quality, perfect for crafting eco-friendly embroidered goods.

Cotton fabric serves as a versatile and reliable medium for embroidery, offering a plethora of benefits and options for creative expression. Whether you're stitching intricate florals

Floral fabric.

Patterned fabric.

on a cotton voile blouse or embellishing denim jeans with geometric patterns, the timeless appeal of cotton ensures that your embroidered creations will be cherished for generations to come.

Embroidering on Knitted Fabrics

You might be unsure about the idea of embroidering on a knitted fabric, but more fabrics are knitted than you might think. For example, T-shirts are often knitted. You can embroider on knitted fabrics, but you just need to be aware of their properties so you can prepare your fabric accordingly or avoid using it if it's not going to be appropriate for your project.

When embroidering on a T-shirt for example, it would be advisable to interface the inside of the garment before you start stitching. If you don't, you will run the risk of pulling the fabric too tight or out of shape during the washing process. Stabilising your fabric with a glue-in woven interfacing will also give it structure, which may be helpful for embroidery appliqué.

Embroidering on knitted fabrics such as jersey and Lycra presents a unique set of challenges for even the most seasoned embroiderers. While these fabrics offer stretch, comfort and versatility in clothing, their inherent properties can make embroidery a delicate balancing act. Let's explore the intricacies of embroidering on knitted fabrics and the considerations every embroiderer should bear in mind.

The Challenges of Embroidering on Knitted Fabrics

- Stretch factor: Knitted fabrics like jersey and Lycra are known for their stretchability, which can pose challenges during the embroidery process. The fabric's elasticity may cause distortion or puckering of the embroidered design, especially if not properly stabilised.
- Fabric texture: The texture of knitted fabrics differs from woven ones, with a more uneven surface that can affect stitch placement and tension. This unevenness may result in inconsistencies in the embroidered design, requiring extra attention to detail and precision.
- Fabric stability: Unlike woven fabrics, knitted fabrics have more inherent movement and stretch, making them prone to shifting during embroidery. Without adequate stabilisation, the fabric may pucker, stretch or distort, compromising the integrity of the embroidered design.
- Thread tension: Achieving the right thread tension is crucial when embroidering on knitted fabrics. The stretchiness of the fabric can affect the tension of the stitches, requiring adjustments to prevent puckering or distortion. Experimentation with thread types and tension settings is often necessary to achieve optimal results.
- Needle selection: Choosing the right needle is paramount when embroidering on knitted fabrics. Sharp needles with a fine point are recommended to pierce the fabric without causing damage or snags. Ballpoint needles are also suitable for knit fabrics, as they slide between the fibres without tearing or stretching the fabric.

Considerations when Embroidering on Fabrics for Clothing

- Fabric type: Different fabrics require different embroidery techniques and considerations. While woven fabrics offer stability and structure, knitted fabrics demand careful attention to stabilisation and handling due to their stretchiness and texture.
- Garment construction: Consider the construction of the garment when planning embroidery placement. Embroidering on pre-assembled garments may limit access to certain areas and require additional precautions to prevent distortion or damage to seams and hems.
- Stabilisation: Proper stabilisation is key to successful embroidery on clothing fabrics, especially knitted ones. Using stabilisers such as cut-away or tear-away backing helps maintain fabric stability and prevents distortion during stitching.
- Test stitching: Before embroidering the final design, it's essential to conduct test stitches on scrap fabric to gauge the fabric's reaction to embroidery and adjust settings accordingly. This allows for fine-tuning of thread tension, stitch density and needle selection to achieve the desired results.
- Care instructions: Consider the garment's care instructions when selecting embroidery techniques and materials. Machine-washable threads and stabilisers are recommended for garments that require frequent washing, ensuring the longevity of the embroidered design.

In summary, embroidering on knitted fabrics like jersey and Lycra presents unique challenges due to their stretchiness, texture and construction. By understanding these challenges and implementing proper techniques and considerations, one can overcome obstacles and achieve beautiful, professional results on clothing fabrics, enhancing garments with intricate and personalised embellishments.

Researching Fabric

Take a trip to fabric shops and haberdasheries, see what is available and take samples if you can. It's not a project as such but start gathering fabric samples and labelling them so you have them to hand. Put them on a ring, so when you start a new project you have a good idea of what is available; having swatches to hand will help with designing and making educated decisions.

Colour can be such a conundrum. The main bit of advice is to get stuck in and try to work with it. Working with colour takes time and experience, so don't put it off. Later in the book we have a whole chapter dedicated to colour, for the simple reason that it is hard to grasp and often you can lack confidence with choosing and pairing colours, mostly through lack of experience.

Choosing your base fabrics is another added layer to your embroidery. While selecting your base, you might ask yourself if it complements your piece or distracts the eye. A top tip would be to choose a pattern or design on the fabric that is either much larger or smaller than the scale of your embroidery, as this will keep the focus on your stitches rather than the background. I have used coloured fabrics and patterns behind my work – it's not easy but if you get it right it can be a delight.

ITEMS YOU WILL NEED

Scissors

Whether you're snipping threads or preparing fabric, scissors are vital. Fabric scissors are key, but if you're not a dressmaker, there's no need to spend a lot. Find a reasonably priced pair; you want them to last but the volume of fabric you will be cutting will not be huge, so they don't need to be top of the range. The key to a well-kept pair of fabric scissors is keeping them only for fabric – never use them for paper or any other material as you will blunt them. Pinking shears are a non-essential but useful pair of scissors. When cutting fabric for embroidery, the pinking shears will limit your fraying edges. The constant movement and touching of fabric during your embroidery project could put your fabric through a little bit of wear, so protecting the edges with a pinking-sheared cut will delay them shedding thread and help prevent embroidery being damaged.

It doesn't stop there when it comes to scissors. Are you going to keep picking up your fabric scissors to cut small threads? You could, but it is not ideal. You have a few options and it will be down to personal preference, so try some out. Snips are great for quick cuts of threads, the simple pinch of your thumb and finger with the snips makes for speedy cutting. You may prefer small embroidery scissors; these long, thin pointed tips are ideal for cutting small threads and getting into awkward areas. Potentially a little sharper and more accurate than a snip.

Needles

- Embroidery/crewel needle: A crewel needle is a medium-length needle with a long eye and a sharp end. It is ideal for piercing tightly woven fabrics and will not leave visible holes.

Top tip: *It's always best to test on the fabric you're using first in case a mark is left.*

- Tapestry needle: This needle is similar to an embroidery needle but it has a blunt end. It is ideal for linen and upholstery fabric where a hole doesn't need to be made.
- Chenille needle: This is a sharp needle, also with a long eye. It is great on most fabrics, especially when working with metallic threads.
- Quilting needles: These are small needles with more rounded eyes. They are best for fine-detail hand stitching as they don't leave holes or cause the fabric to fray. They are used a lot in hand quilting, hence the name.

It is really down to personal preference so try them out and if your budget allows, make all the options available for yourself.

Thimbles (Confessions of a Thimble Addict)

Do you need them? Maybe you're thinking they are a bit outdated and not essential. Trust me, once you have used them you will not look back. They come in different sizes and materials; metal, rubber and even porcelain. Again, it's down to preference. The beauty of a thimble is that it gives you protection and therefore speed in your work. When using a thimble, the back end of the needle is not compromising the skin on your finger. If you take time to try some out and get the one that is best for you, it's worth using. Sometimes I stitch without if I have misplaced my favourites, but I soon regret it as my fingertips will need days to recover from repetitively pushing the needle through the fabric. You may find the fabric you have chosen has a tighter weave or you want to use a slightly thicker thread. Both of these factors will make a difference to how easy or hard it is to pull the thread through the fabric. It may depend a little on your style of stitching, but if you're building up stitches in one area it will become increasingly taxing to pull the thread through your work, meaning some parts of your project will need a little extra force behind the needle.

For me, working without a thimble feels like I'm naked! There, I said it.

Quick Unpick

This is a great tool for undoing mistakes and cutting tiny stitches out of your work.

Sketchbooks and Notebooks

I think an essential part of developing is making notes or having a sketchbook to hand to jot down things you want to do when you think of them, or to remind you of things to avoid next time. Equally you don't want to forget an inspirational idea part-way through a task. Sketchbooks are a vital tool if you want to be designing and creating your own ideas ready to stitch; sometimes the best ideas hit at unexpected times so always carry a small sketchbook just in case.

Air-Soluble Drawing Pencils and Markers

Drawing tools to mark your fabric are key but this will be down to preference; not all projects will need the same tool, so have a wide range of mark-making tools for your designs. The embroidery pencil enables you to draw freehand onto the fabric and trace off designs using a light source – a window or light box. An embroidery pencil will fade over time so if you make a mistake drawing up your design, you need not worry about it sticking around. The negative is that it will fade; you may want to use a regular pencil for long-term projects so your marks remain on the fabric.

My preferred tool is a regular drawing pencil, as it gives the definition and fine line I need to draw up my designs. It lasts on the fabric for large projects. If you know your lines will definitely be covered on your fabric, you can also use a pen as it will not be rubbed off or fade, but this is risky if you might change or edit a design part way through. Papers are also available that you can print your design on, stick on the fabric and then stitch over the top. When your design is complete, you dissolve the paper in water. (I don't cover this option here as it is a different style of stitching.)

Heat Pens

A heat pen is a great tool to have in your kit. Like the embroidery pencil, the marks are not permanent. Unlike the pencil which will fade after a while, the heat pens require you to apply heat from an iron in order to make the marks vanish.

Transfer Paper and Embossers

Later in the book we talk about transferring images and explore different techniques. It's worth testing out some transfer papers and embossing tools. They will be extremely important if you're transferring a detailed design to fabric.

Light Box

Do you really need one? Not necessarily, as a sunny window can be great. But for the times you don't want to be holding up an image and juggling things up against the window, a light box is worth getting. You can buy reasonably priced light pads that are battery operated and often come with different brightness settings. If you need to trace off with a light source regularly, it's worth the purchase.

Pins and Masking Tape

These are both essential to transferring an image. Masking tape is great for keeping an image in place on a source without leaving a mark, and great for blocking out an area if you choose to incorporate paint with embroidery. Pins can also be a very reliable way to keep an image in place whilst you transfer.

Ruler and Tape Measure

I cannot work without either a tape measure or a ruler. You may find you need these more than you thought; you will need it to measure fabric but also when marking up a design to check it's central or straight. I have invested in a pattern-cutter's marking ruler – it's brilliant. It makes measuring so simple as it has right angles and is made of clear plastic, which makes measuring things on fabric or paper a dream.

Hoops and Stretcher Bars

One of the most important parts of the prepping process is stretching your fabric ready for embroidering on. If you do this badly, you can compromise the quality of your embroidery. If your fabric is stretched and pulled tight into

Hoops come in a variety of sizes and shapes. They can be made of plastic, metal or wood.

a hoop it should sound like a drum. Being ready to stitch on a well-prepped fabric will give you clean results and the stitching process will be much more enjoyable.

What are you stretching your fabric on? There are several ways of doing this and it will vary depending on your project. For larger pieces you can stretch your fabric onto an embroidery frame, which allows you to roll it as you are working on different sections, giving you the opportunity to create large pieces whilst keeping the fabric held tightly so it doesn't pucker and frustrate you at the framing stage. If you're working on a small project you may choose to select a hoop and stretch your fabric, which may stay in the hoop for presentation. Hoops come in many sizes, can be wooden, plastic and occasionally metal, and vary widely in design, shape and colour. Most hoops are round, but you can find oval and rounded square shapes too. Hoops are normally sized in inches and have an adjuster at the top to increase the tension. This will be down to personal preference and the nature of the project. I would recommend a lightweight bamboo hoop to start with, but some thicker fabrics may pair best with a heavier, stronger hoop in wood or plastic.

After many years of embroidery practice, my favourite way to embroider when stitching a wall piece is to buy wooden stretcher bars from an art supplier and then stretch my preferred fabric. This works similarly to a hoop but you have autonomy over size and fabric, the frame is stronger and more substantial. However, stretching your fabric over the bars can be a challenge; it takes time and a bit of practice, which we will cover in Chapter 8.

Threads

So this is when we get to the fun part – threads are amazing. When you start buying threads, how big is your collection going to be? How many threads will you need to complete your collection? How long is a piece of thread? Welcome to the world of threads, from metallics, stranded cotton, organic, naturally dyed, tapestry wool, cotton pearl, silk and satin. The possibilities are endless once you start choosing colour palettes.

Thread storage.

Threads.

Choosing your threads is the best bit; threads can bring your work to life. What you choose for each project will give a different texture and finish to every piece.

If you're new to embroidery or looking for a very wide variety of colours in your work, a standard cotton skein is a very versatile, reliable thread to embroider with. This is my go-to. You get a great finish. The special thing about a standard cotton skein is that it is split into six threads. This gives you the opportunity to use anywhere from one to six threads at a time, giving you a very fine to a substantially chunky stitch. You can use this versatility within one embroidery piece; it's a very adaptable thread and this is what I mostly use. When using other yarn and thread, be sure to test it on your fabric first, experiment with fabric types and needle sizes, and ask yourself what is going to give you the best results.

Storage

Keeping your supplies and potentially a work area clear and tidy is not always easy, and becomes more frustrating if you have limited time to embroider. It is quite challenging to make time to embroider and first have to locate all your tools and get everything in order. Organising your threads and tools is key. You can do this on a budget and you don't need fancy equipment. My workspace is in my North London home, so space is limited and I always need to clear away my things so as not to interrupt family life. The great thing is that embroidery does not require a lot of room; you just need a space for your threads, fabric and a few hoops. This can all be contained in a small box or bag. The beauty of it is you can stitch on your lap, carry it around, travel anywhere with it. Organise yourself for an enjoyable embroidery experience; you need to try a few things to see what works best for you.

I used to store all my equipment in an old bureau, as everything was quickly accessible and I could tidy away as easily as lifting the lid. This was great for a while, but my tools and equipment now exceed the space and I have taken over a large understairs cupboard with my supplies and past work. The most important part of addressing my storage situation has been to organise my vast variety of threads into a set of drawers that I have sectioned off. Each drawer has dividers for threads according to colours. You can purchase thread boxes and they are a great storage solution. I very much wanted my threads out in my living space, but not getting in the way of our home decor. Some people use wooden pegs to wind their thread on, then put them on display. Threads can be wound on plastic bobbins then hooped on metal rings in groups of colours. If you only organise one element, make your threads a priority.

The best thing to do is to research fabric and try to test out as much of the embroidery equipment as you can. Here is a beginner's project to get your teeth into. This will hopefully inspire you to get your kit ready and decide how best to store it.

Organised threads.

The finished needle book.

MAKE A NEEDLE BOOK

You will need:

Two rectangular pieces of fabric measuring 10cm × 18cm
One piece of rectangular fabric measuring 6.5cm × 18cm, folded in half and pressed
A piece of ribbon 30cm long
Two pieces of fusible interfacing measuring 10cm × 18cm
9cm × 17cm felt folded in half, for pages in your book
Pins
Scissors
Embroidery pen/marking pen
Snips

Step 1

Cut and prep your fabric. Take your 10cm × 18cm fabric and fold it in half longways, press this in half and this will become your pocket. Set this to one side. Take up your fusible interfacing and your fabric, placing your fabric right side down on to a flat surface. Iron on your fusible interfacing to the wrong side of your fabric, repeat this for both rectangles of fabric. Turn over and press on the right side as well to ensure the fusible interfacing has glued to your fabric.

Step 2

Pin your fabric. Take your 13cm × 18cm rectangular pieces of fabric and lay on top of the piece you folded.

Step 3

The folded line should sit lengthways to match the length of your fabric, with the folded line sitting around halfway down your fabric.

Prep the fabric and ribbon for the needle book.

Fold over and top stitch the top edge of the pocket piece.

Step 4
Pin your pocket into place.

Step 5
You then attach your ribbon just above the fold line on both the left and right side of your fabric, at this point it will run from left to right in place but the ribbon is too long. Find the centre of the ribbon and cut in half – if you do this whilst it's attached either side you can be sure they are even on each side. Make sure the ribbons are out of the line of sewing. Next pin on top the fused fabric that remains, ensuring you pin them right side to right side. Pin all the way around, so it can't move when you start sewing.

Fold over and top stitch the top edge of the pocket piece.

Step 6
If you have a sewing machine, you can sew this up with a seam allowance of around 8mm. You can do a back stitch by hand if you don't have a machine – it will take longer but you will be proud of the results. Sew all the way around leaving a small gap so you can turn out the needle book.

Take your time to push the corners out, you can gently use a pencil but be careful not to push through the seam at this point, creating a hole. If you remove the pencil sometimes a wiggle of the corners between your fingertips will help the fabric work its way into a clean pointed corner.

Then press your book – this is key before you top-stitch the booklet. At the opening, tuck in the raw fabric so your sewn line continues neatly, with 0.5cm top-stitch around your booklet.

Place the fabric right side to right side with the ribbons sandwiched inside and the pocket in place.

Step 7
Place your felt in the middle of your book, find the centre and pin in place in the book ready to sew. Sew your felt pages down the centre and your booklet is ready to place your needles on the pages, a small pair of snips and perhaps your needle threader in the pocket.

Once the fabric has been turned through, top stitch the edges approximately 0.3cm from the edge all the way around the booklet.

Use scraps of fabric or even fabric from old clothes to make these needle books. If you have pinking shears, you can cut the felt pages with these for a nice finish.

During some embroidery projects you may need a variety of needles or even a supply of the same size with different colour thread ready to go. This little needle book is a handy way to keep your needles in one place, and a great way to transport your needles if you take your embroidery on your travels with you. The exciting bit is choosing fabric that represents you and your style.

Stitch in the pre-cut felt pages.

MAKE A UTILITY WRAP

Like the mini needle book, another great way to stay organised and have tidy and efficiently stored supplies is to make yourself a utility wrap. Embossing tools, pencils, scissors and embroidery pens can all be stored in this tidy wrap. A utility wrap can be made from calico or drill, denim or canvas. Choose something sturdy. Using second-hand fabrics from jeans and jackets is a fun way to recycle and to make your wrap personalised.

You will need:
Ruler
Pencil
Pins
Binding or trim
A sewing machine
Ribbon
Thick cotton, drill or calico
Embroidery pencil/tailor's chalk

Step 1
Cut one rectangle the same size, around 45 cm x 45 cm.

Cut one piece 45cm x 15cm.

Cut a length of bias binding to generously fit around the edges of the utility wrap. This should be around 185cm. (You can cut off the excess, or continue to sew it around the wrap.)

Cut a piece of ribbon to 30cm (you can then cut to size when the wrap is finished).

Step 2
Using the binding, edge the middle sized and the smallest fabric along the top raw edges. This is an effective way to finish an edge without the need to 'bag out' (turn the piece inside out once sewn).

Step 3
Now your strips for your pockets have been prepared, place the middle-sized fabric on top of the largest piece and pin in place so the bottom edges meet. With tailor's chalk or an embroidery pencil, mark at a right angle to the bottom edge where you want pockets to be, make them snug enough but not so tight that it's a struggle to get things out. Stitching the pockets around 2.5cm is good for pencils and pens. You may want them to vary if you want to roll up scissors in the wrap. Lay your tools on top and mark how big you want each pocket. Once you're happy with your marked pockets, stitch the middle strip to the base strip down the pocket lines with a machine.

Step 4
Add the next pocket. For those items that need storing but are shorter, use the second strip, the smallest one, to create some shallow pockets. Try to stitch some pockets in the same place as the layer before so no pockets are interrupted by stitch lines.

Step 5
Place the ribbons on one side of the wrap around halfway up the edge of the fabric, keeping the raw edges of the ribbon against the raw edge of the fabric so the ribbon should be laying on top of your pocket panels, then pin. Now complete the raw edge of your wrap with a bias binding, making sure to catch the ribbons attached at the side.

Press the wrap and trim any excess threads.

Ta da! You have finished your utility wrap!

It's ready to hold all your embroidery tools and have them neatly accessible in one place. Place the tools in the wrap and roll up your fabric with everything safely tucked inside.

Both these projects are a great way to get started on organising your things and making your own storage; it will make accessing your equipment easy and you can work with clarity. Both these projects could be customised later when you have mastered a few stitches. They also make great gifts for friends and family if they enjoy embroidering or are interested in starting.

Cut and prep the fabric.

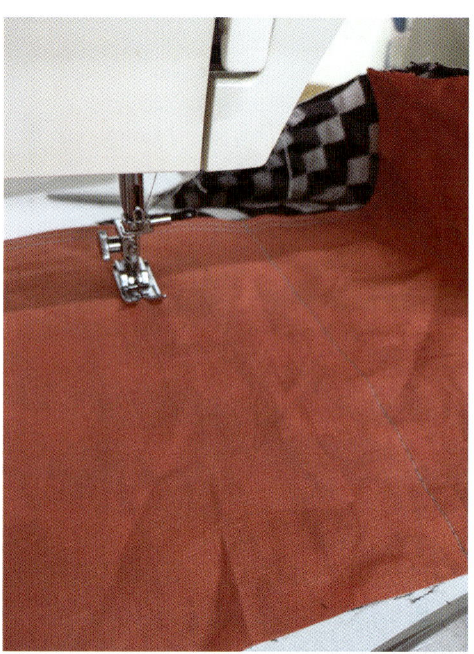

Stitch the pocket to the main base with vertical lines by hand or machine, leaving enough space in each pocket for utensils.

Sew down the pockets, and hem with machine or by hand.

Use bias binding to hem the whole wrap. Remember to include the wrap tie.

Now you're kitted out with a very useful and handy place to keep your sewing utensils.

CHAPTER 2

ON YOUR MARK MAKING, GET SET, GO!

Now your tools are ready and you have explored some fabric options, you're ready to get going. Learning to be comfortable with your needle and thread will be key to developing your skills and freeing your love of embroidery. It will give you confidence to carve out your unique style and approach. Once you know the basics like the back of your hand, your creativity will evolve. Your time will not be spent on getting the stitches right; instead they should become second nature so that you can make choices in an instant and enhance your work. As you practise and become familiar, you will discover the things you like most and your preferences will aid your design process and give you the best results.

In order to freestyle and become at one with your needle and thread, you need to put in the time and practice. Like anything, practice will give you more knowledge of your tools and techniques and how to best use them. Don't be surprised if as you finish a project, you see its faults; you may not even want to look at your previous creations. Sometimes this is helpful, it's a good sign you are growing and want to progress. Be prepared to make mistakes and learn from them.

Before mastering any technical stitch, a great introduction to embroidery is to get familiar with your tools. In the previous chapter we talked about the range of tools available

Mark making in pinks and oranges.

Mark making.

and finding the ones that suit you. The best way to find this out is by starting to use them. If you're not enjoying them, switch things up.

An artist makes marks on a canvas; they may be a collection of lines that make up an abstract composition. An artist also makes a series of varying marks on a canvas and can make a comprehensive image whether life-like or impressionist. The marks collectively form a familiar shape or image for the viewer. The aim of these mark-making projects is to help you master your techniques. You will learn a variety of stitches, the equivalent to a painter changing their brushes and mark-making tools. In embroidery your thread and needle remain pretty standard. The needle goes into the fabric and out the other side, followed by a line of thread, be it metallic or standard cotton; the change is the stitch you can use to create texture and definition. Experiment with it and find your style.

This chapter will take you step by step through the key stitches you will need as an embroiderer. Below is a list of tools you will need for mastering these technical stitches.

The tools you will need to get you started.

TECHNICAL STITCH INSTRUCTIONS

These step-by-step instructions will give you all you need to start practising some basic stitch techniques. They will give you the stepping stones to propel you into finding your style.

You will need:
Embroidery hoop
Fabric (ideally an embroidery fabric like cotton or linen)
Embroidery floss (stranded cotton thread)
Embroidery needle (usually a sharp or crewel needle)
Scissors
Pencil/embroiderer's pencil
Ruler
Thimble

These stitches are to test out and practise at your own pace – at this point you are not under any pressure for your stitches to be perfect or for there to be an end product. Simply follow the instructions and practise.

Running Stitch

Embroidering a running stitch is one of the simplest and most basic hand embroidery techniques. It's often used for outlining and creating fine lines in embroidery designs. Here's a step-by-step guide on how to embroider a running stitch.

Step 1
Place your fabric in an embroidery hoop. This helps keep the fabric taut and makes stitching easier. Tighten the hoop screw to secure the fabric.

Step 2
Cut a length of embroidery floss (approximately 40cm–50cm) and separate the strands. A typical embroidery floss strand consists of six smaller strands, but you can use fewer strands for a thinner line if desired. For practising this stitch, use three strands. Thread the strands through the eye of the embroidery needle and tie a knot at the other end to create a single-threaded strand with a knot at one end.

Step 3
Draw a line, with a ruler or freehand. As this is a practice project, it's about getting used to the motion and step-by-step repetition of the instructions. Start at the beginning of your line.

Step 4
Insert the needle, bring the needle up from the back side of the fabric to the front at the starting point.

Step 5
Decide on the direction of your running stitch (in this case you're covering your drawn line). Typically, you'll work from left to right, but you can also work from right to left or in any other direction based on your design.

Make the first stitch by inserting the needle back into the fabric from the front, creating a straight stitch. The length of this stitch is up to you, but it should be consistent for a neat look. To make your next stitch, you will be leaving a space similar to the one created by the thread.

Step 6
Continue making stitches in the same direction, evenly spaced along your design line. Each time you make a stitch, the needle should go down and come up slightly ahead, forming a continuous line of stitches. To secure the last stitch, insert the needle from the front to the back at the end point of your line. Flip the fabric to the back side and tie a knot with the loose end of the thread around the existing stitches. Trim any excess thread.

Remember to keep your stitches even in length and spacing for a clean and uniform running stitch. Practice is key to improving your embroidery skills, so don't be discouraged if your first attempts aren't perfect. With time and patience, you'll become more proficient at creating beautiful running stitch designs. To practise this stitch, try drawing a circle, wavy line or an organic shape and stitch along. Vary your stitch lengths on each line and you can experiment with changing up the number of strands of thread.

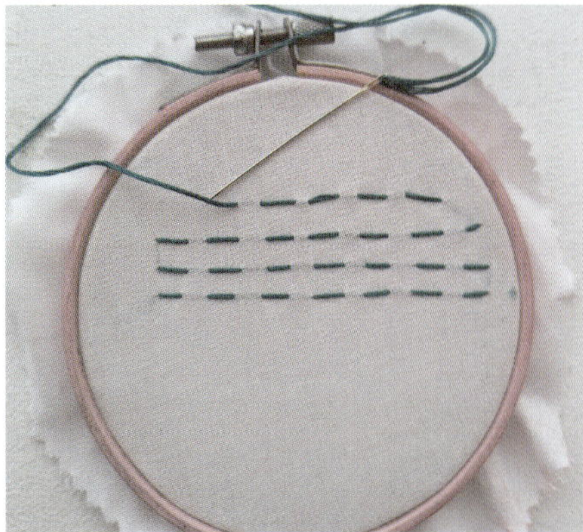

Running stitch.

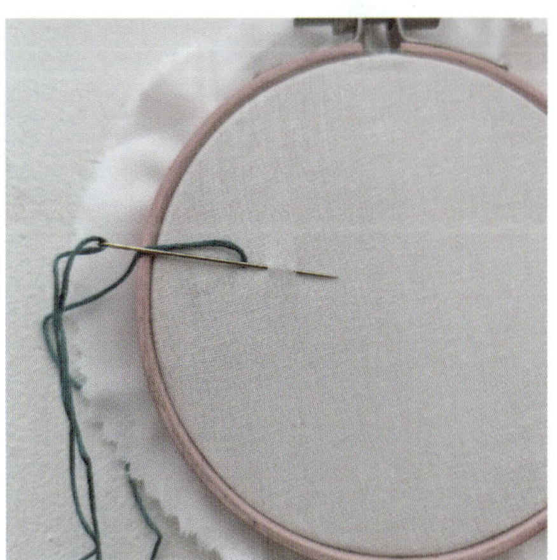

Starting the running stitch.

Back Stitch

Embroidering a back stitch is a fundamental hand embroidery technique that creates a solid and continuous line of stitching. It's commonly used for outlining and adding fine details in embroidery projects.

Step 1
Place your fabric in your hoop. Remember to tighten the hoop so the fabric sits firmly held. If the fabric has some slack, it will become harder to stitch and compromise the finished look. Separate the desired number of embroidery floss strands (usually two to three; if you tried three on the previous stitch practice, try two), thread them through the eye of your embroidery needle and knot the other end of the floss to secure it. Draw a line as a guide for your stitching.

Step 2
Start from the back. Bring the needle up from the back of the fabric at the starting point of your design. This is typically at the end of the line you want to embroider.

Step 3
Decide on the length of your first stitch. This can vary depending on your design, but a typical starting point is around 3mm–6mm. Insert the needle back into the fabric, making sure it's a little behind the starting point (the distance should be equal to the desired stitch length). The needle should exit on the same line you're creating.

Step 4
Complete the first stitch. Pull the needle and thread through the fabric until the knot at the end of the floss stops it. You

Back stitch.

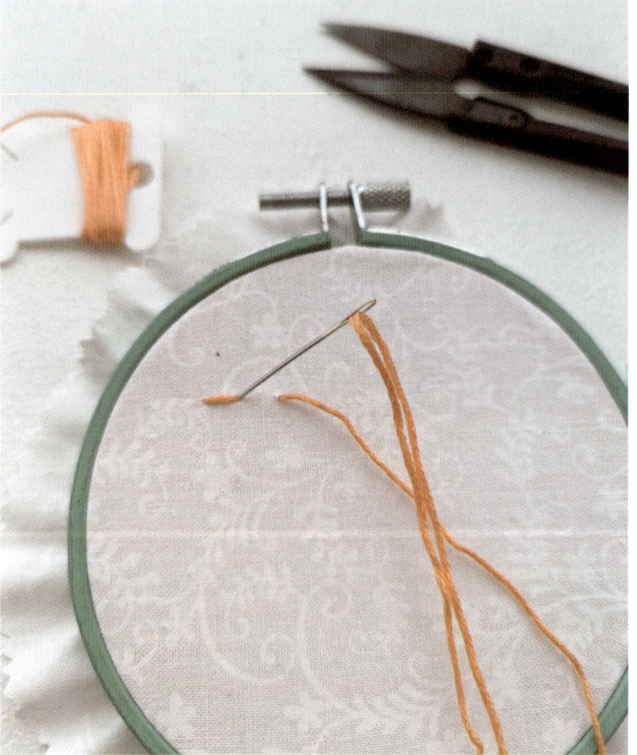

now have your first back stitch. It should look like a straight line on the front of the fabric.

Step 5
To create the next stitch, bring the needle up from the fabric a short distance ahead (equal to your desired stitch length). Insert the needle back into the fabric at the end of the previous stitch.

Step 6
Repeat this process for each subsequent stitch, always bringing the needle up ahead and inserting it back into the fabric at the end of the previous stitch.

Step 7
When you've completed your back stitch line, bring the needle to the back side of the fabric and secure it with a small knot. You can do this by taking a tiny stitch on the back, then passing the needle through the loop before pulling it tight.

It's as simple as that. With practice, you can make even and precise lines, and you can use this technique for various embroidery projects including lettering, outlines and decorative details. Take the time to draw up a variety of lines to practise stitching along.

Pull the needle through the fabric and enter back into the fabric approximately 0.5cm.

From under your fabric, bring your needle back up to the top of your fabric, the same length of your first stitch. Enter the fabric back through the last hole that your last stitch went through. You have created a back stitch, which you can then repeat along the line.

Split Stitch

Embroidering a split stitch is a basic and versatile technique that can be used for outlining, filling and adding texture to your embroidery projects. Follow the step-by-step guide to master the split stitch.

Step 1
Start by securing your fabric in the embroidery hoop. This keeps the fabric taut and makes it easier to work on. Separate the embroidery floss into two or three strands (depending on the thickness you want). Thread your needle with the desired number of strands and tie a knot at the end.

Step 2
Plan your design. Draw a line – this can be a straight line or if you're feeling more confident with your needle and thread, you can start with a freehand line.

Step 3
Bring your needle up from the back of the fabric to the front at the starting point of your design. Insert your needle back into the fabric, very close to where it emerged. This will create a single straight stitch.

Step 4
Before pulling your needle all the way through, pass it up through the middle of the straight stitch you just created. This will split the stitch in half.

Step 5
Continue working in the same manner, creating a single straight stitch and then splitting it, as you move along your design. Make sure to keep your stitches even in length. When you reach the end of your design or want to finish the line, bring your needle to the back of the fabric and secure it with a knot. Trim any excess thread.

Split stitch.

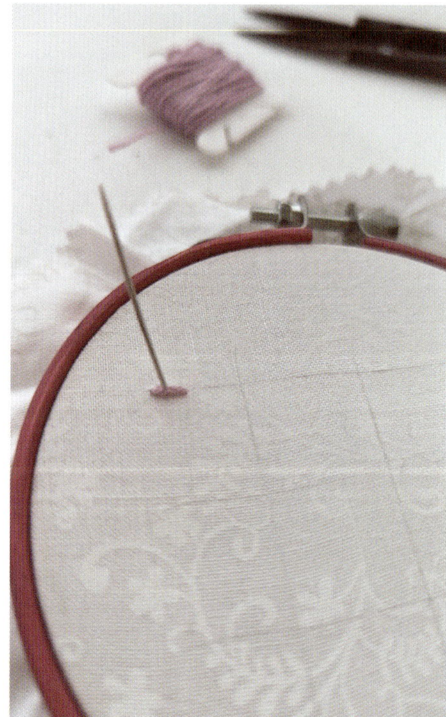

First step, first stitch.

Split stitching can take some practice to get the hang of, especially if you're new to embroidery. Don't be discouraged if your first attempts don't look perfect; with practice, your stitches will become neater and more consistent. Remember you can vary the stitch lengths to create texture, you can experiment with different thread colours and thicknesses to create your desired look, and over time you will develop your own style using split stitch.

Split the stitch.

Put your needle through the middle of the stitch you have just made and pull it through.

Satin Stitch

Embroidering a satin stitch is a beautiful way to add smooth, glossy and solid areas of colour to your projects. Satin stitch can add a shiny, polished appearance and is often used for filling in designs. Changing direction within a filled space can also add texture to your piece. Once you have practised the stitch, try experimenting with the thickness of thread and stitch direction.

Step 1

Start with a clean, ironed piece of fabric. Secure in an embroidery hoop, making sure it's taut but not overly stretched. Draw a shape; simply try a circle, triangle or square, or if you're feeling confident you could draw an organic or a recognisable shape, for example an apple, a heart or a star. Choose the design you want to embroider and mark it on the fabric using a water-soluble fabric marker or embroidery pencil.

Create your stitch by pulling the needle up through and back into the fabric, according to the shape you are stitching.

Satin stitch.

Make sure your design lines are clear and accurate. This will help with the finish of your stitches. Separate the embroidery floss into the desired number of strands. Thread your needle with the floss and knot the end. Bring your needle up from the back of the fabric at one edge of the area you want to fill with satin stitch.

Step 2

Insert the needle back down into the fabric close to where you came up. Make sure the stitch is parallel to the design lines.

Bring the needle back up again just beside the first stitch, leaving no gaps between the stitches. Continue stitching parallel lines, keeping them close together. The stitches should be of equal length and evenly spaced.

Step 3

Pay close attention to the direction and angle of your stitches. For a polished satin stitch, try to keep the stitches as parallel and as close together as possible.

Needle up through the fabric.

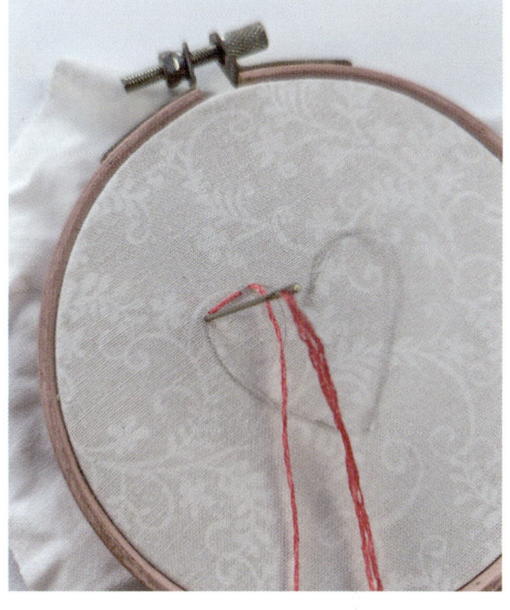

Back into fabric.

Keep your tension consistent, neither too loose nor too tight. Continue stitching until you have filled the entire area within your design lines.

Step 4
When you reach the end of the area or need to finish the stitch, make sure the final stitch is neatly placed. To secure your thread, bring the needle to the back of the fabric. Tie a knot on the back or weave the thread through nearby stitches on the back of the fabric to secure it. Trim any excess thread.

Step 5
Pressing your embroidery will give a beautiful finish, it's great to practise this while you're getting the hang of stitches and good practice going forward. After removing any markings and securing the threads, gently press your embroidery on the reverse side with a low-heat iron. This will help set the stitches and make your satin stitch area appear smoother.

It may take a while to master the satin stitch; don't be discouraged at your first few attempts – you will soon discover the best approach for you.

Back up through the fabric next to previous stitch.

French Knot

A French knot is a basic technique that can be used to create textured and decorative elements in your embroidery projects. Once you have grasped the basics, you can adjust your thread thickness to create varying texture within your work.

Step 1
Start by securing your fabric in an embroidery hoop. Select the colour of embroidery floss you want to use and separate out one or two strands from the bundle. Most embroidery floss consists of six strands twisted together, you can adjust the thickness by using fewer strands.

Step 2
Thread your chosen number of strands through the eye of your embroidery needle. Make sure the thread is long enough for your intended knot and leave a tail of a few inches. Start on the front side of your fabric where you want to create the French knot. Pull the needle up from the back side to the front, leaving the tail end of the thread on the back.

Bring the needle up through the fabric.

French knots.

Step 3
Hold the needle in your right hand and use your left hand to hold the thread taut above the fabric, about 5cm from where the needle came up. With the needle in your right hand, wrap the thread around the needle two to three times. The more wraps you make, the larger the French knot will be.

Step 4
Hold the wraps firmly in place with your left hand while you insert the needle back into the fabric, right next to where it originally came up.

Step 5
Gently push the needle down through the fabric while keeping the wraps secure with your left hand. Be careful not to pull the wraps too tight, or the knot may become too small.

Wrap the thread around the needle according to the size of knot you want.

Push the needle back through the same hole it came up through.

Wrap the thread three times around the needle.

The finished French knot.

Step 6

After inserting the needle completely, pull it all the way through to the back of the fabric. This will form the French knot. Secure the knot by gently tugging on the tail of the thread on the back side of the fabric to tighten the knot against the fabric. Trim any excess thread from both the front and back of the fabric, leaving a short tail. Then repeat. Remember the size of knot and number of wraps can be adjusted to suit your project design.

The French knot is a tricky stitch – keep practising until you find you are satisfied with your technique. Like the previous stitch practices, draw yourself a shape and fill it with French knots. The repetitive nature of filling a space with these beautiful tiny knots will help you gain confidence and perfection.

Chain Stitch

Embroidering a chain stitch is a fundamental and versatile embroidery technique that can be used for outlining, filling and creating decorative patterns in your embroidery projects. Here's a step-by-step guide on how to embroider a basic chain stitch.

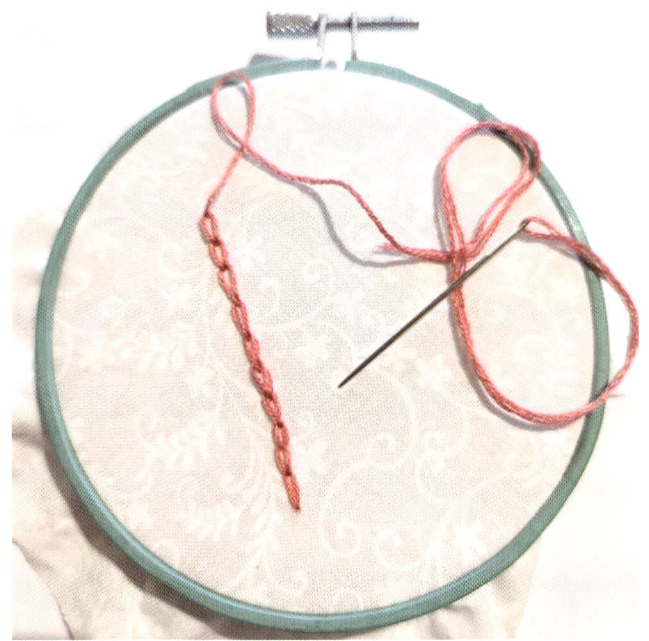

Chain stitch.

Step 1

Make sure the fabric is stretched smoothly within the hoop, without any wrinkles or puckers. You may want to draw a line to follow whilst you're practising this stitch.

Thread your embroidery needle with the desired colour of thread. You can use a single strand for a delicate chain stitch or multiple strands for a thicker and more prominent stitch.

Thread your needle, tie a knot in the end of your thread. Bring your needle up through the back of the fabric at the starting point of your line. This is typically where you want to create the first chain stitch. To create the first loop, insert the needle back into the fabric, very close to where it came out, but leave a small loop of thread on the surface.

Step 2

To secure, pass the needle through the loop from the underside to the top. This loop should look like the first link in a chain.

Step 3

To create subsequent chain stitches, repeat the process. Bring the needle up from the back slightly ahead of where the first chain stitch ended (this is where your next stitch will begin). Insert the needle back into the fabric near the exit point of the previous stitch, leaving a loop again. Secure the new loop by passing the needle through the loop you just created, from the underside to the top.

Step 4

Continue making chain stitches, ensuring that the loops are of consistent size and shape for a neat appearance. To finish your chain stitch, secure the last loop by passing the needle through it, but this time, do not come up on the fabric surface.

Pull the needle through the fabric and push it back through the same hole, leaving a loop.

Bring the needle back up through the fabric, catching the loop in place and pulling the loop tight.

Repeat the process to form a chain.

Step 5

Turn your fabric over to the back side and tie a small knot with the thread end to secure it. Trim any excess thread.

Practice is key to achieving uniform and beautiful chain stitches. Experiment with different thread thicknesses and colours to create various effects.

Now you are fully confident in knowing what each stitch does and how to create them, it's good practice to put them all together and start experimenting. Playing and experimenting with embroidery stitches will inspire you for future freehand projects. A great way to bring together the techniques you have learnt so far in this book is to undertake a small project, that way you will start to form a style for yourself and increasingly know how best you work and what you like (or don't like) about embroidery. You may already have your favourites from the few stitches you have learnt so far. You may also be inspired to adapt and add to the basics.

Creating a finished piece from this chapter will give you a sense of achievement and start you on your journey of self-designed embroidery.

SMALL MARK-MAKING HOOP

You will need:
Embroidery hoop – choose a hoop of your preferred size (smaller hoops are easier for beginners).
Fabric – select a piece of fabric that suits your project, light-coloured, plain cotton or linen fabric is a good choice for beginners.
Embroidery floss – gather a variety of embroidery floss colours, choose from a single brand's colour palette or mix and match different brands for a unique look.
Embroidery needles – use embroidery needles with a sharp point and a large eye, which makes it easier to thread the floss.
Scissors – sharp embroidery scissors for cutting thread.
Marking tools – water-soluble fabric markers or a light pencil to draw your design on the fabric.

Basic tools are required for this project; a selection of threads, needles, snips and embroidery pencil along with your fabric and hoop.

Step 1
Cut the fabric to a size that fits comfortably within your embroidery hoop, leaving at least 5cm around the outside of the hoop so you have enough fabric to finish and neaten your finished piece. Stretch the fabric tightly over the inner hoop, place the outer hoop over it, and tighten the screw to secure it. Make sure the fabric is smooth and taut. When you tap it, it should be drum-like. Adjust if needs be.

Playing with stitches on a small mark-making hoop.

Hoop up the fabric.

Step 2

Design your canvas. This can be daunting; the best approach is to get started, remember you are covering your fabric in stitches, if you want to change your design part way through that is OK.

Sketch your desired mark-making pattern on the fabric using a fabric marker or a light pencil. Make this an abstract design, simple shapes, or even just lines and curves. This will give you the chance to concentrate on the mark making rather than the composition or subject. Think of including circles, semicircles, squares, arches, ovals and other two-dimensional shapes. Remember you're not looking to fill all the shapes; your aim is to try to use the variety of stitches you have learnt. It may mean a simple running stitch in a circle is good practice for using a running stitch on a curved line.

Step 3

Choose a colour palette that suits your project. For an experimental approach, you can select contrasting or complementary colours. Experiment with thread thickness by using multiple strands of embroidery floss. You can separate the strands and use two to six strands together, depending on your desired effect.

Step 4

Decide which basic embroidery stitches you want to use. Some stitches to consider include:

- Back stitch: Good for outlining and creating precise lines.
- Running stitch: Creates dashed lines and is great for texture.
- Satin stitch: Fills in shapes with smooth, solid colour.
- French knot: Adds texture and dimension.
- Seed stitch: Creates a speckled texture. Embrace.

Step 5

Start with a section of your design and experiment with different stitches, thread thicknesses and colours. Try varying the length and spacing of your stitches for added texture and uniqueness. Don't be afraid to make mistakes or change your mind. The beauty of an experimental project is embracing imperfections and surprises.

Draw up a simple lines-and-shapes design on the hooped fabric. Do this with an embroidery pencil.

Step 6

Begin stitching your design according to your plan or allow your experimentation to guide you. Keep your stitches neat and consistent, but don't worry too much about perfection. If you are new to embroidery you may need to take regular breaks – it may take longer than anticipated.

Step 7

Once you are satisfied the mark-making embroidery hoop is finished, tie off and trim any excess threads on the bottom of your hoop. Trim any excess fabric, leaving about an inch around your design.

Using a running stitch and a full six threads (it needs to be strong), pull the thread through on the excess fabric approximately 3cm away from the hoop edge. Stitch around the outside of the hoop, until you return to the starting point. Do not cut your thread at this point, gently pull the thread so that the running stitches gather up your excess fabric snugly to the back of your hoop. Tie a secure knot to the fabric so the gathers are held in place. You can now leave the back as is or glue a piece of felt or fabric to cover it for a cleaner look. Later there will be an example in the book of how to sew the back felt on to the hoop.

All done! Your experimental mark-making embroidery project is ready to be displayed in your hoop or framed as wall art.

Remember, the key to an experimental project is to enjoy the process and let your creativity flow. Don't be afraid to take risks and try new things. Your project will be a unique reflection of your artistic expression. If you found it helpful, repeat with new colours and shapes. This is also a great way, between projects, to feel released to experiment and find new ideas.

Start practising stitch techniques along the line and in the shapes.

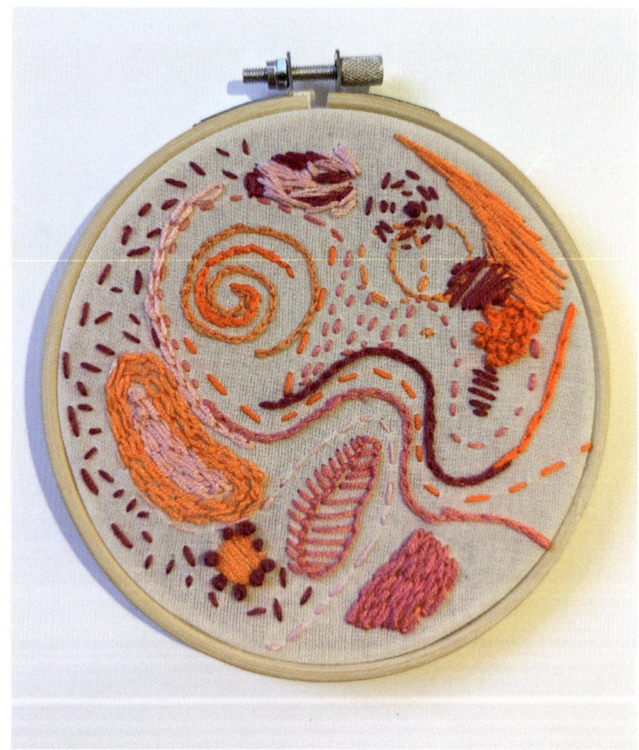

The completed mark-making hoop.

WALL HANGING PROJECT

So, you have learnt how to do some key basic stitches and you have potentially created your first hoop. This is a great way to get your hand in, finding your own way with how you stitch. Here is a larger project for you to take a longer time over; it will give you a challenge to start thinking about composition and displaying your finished work. What would you want to put on your walls, or give as a gift? When you have a customer or audience to consider you will be questioning your choices in a much more considered way. This can help you think about what colours to choose for your piece, without over-complicating it. There are helpful tools online to help find great colour palettes, if putting colours together is not a strong point. Later in the book we will go into depth about colour theory, how to select colours to help your work come to life. For this project, a wall hanging, it's about fully finding your feet with your stitches and feeling comfortable and inspired to stitch. Knowing the basics well will give you a great foundation on which to build your own style.

You will need:

Rectangular pieces of fabric (a thicker cotton such as drill or canvas, but a linen could be delightful), approximately 35cm × 45cm
Scissors
Threads in your chosen colour palette
Needle
2cm wooden dowel
Pencil/embroidery pencil or marker

Step 1

Cut approximately A3 size pieces of fabric 35cm × 45cm; this will give you enough around the edge for a seam allowance so you can finish your wall hanging to a quality standard. Measure your piece to around 34cm (plus 1.5cm each side for seam allowance) × 43cm (with 1.5 cm each side for seam allowance). As it's a wall hanging, you want a reasonably thick fabric like a drill, canvas or heavyweight calico, not so thick that it's hard to stitch but enough so it has some weight to it for hanging.

Wall hanging project.

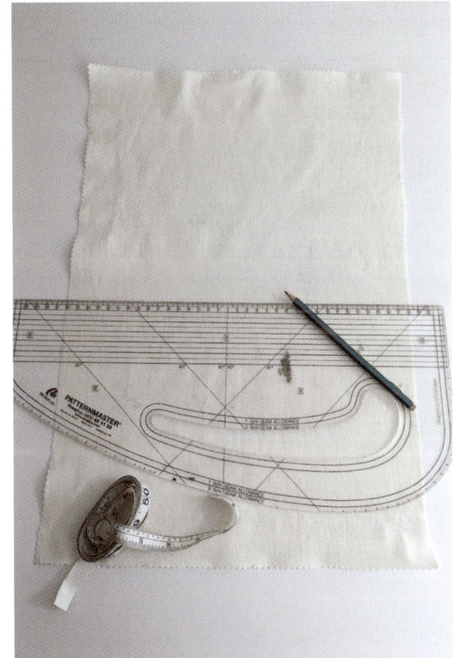

Measure out the fabric you need for the wall-hanging project.

Step 2
Draw on simple shapes and lines with a standard or embroidery pencil, compose an abstract design that you want to display and are excited to stitch. Think about the space between the lines; you may have areas of concentrated stitches and emptier spaces, take a step back to check the composition of your lines before you start stitching. If you stick with less shapes, you can always add more later – it will be harder to erase the shapes if you feel it's crowded.

Draw up the wall-hanging design using simple shapes and lines.

Step 3
Select your colour palette. Don't over complicate it. I think about six to ten colours are enough, with a range of darker, stronger colours and a mix of mid tones and light shades. Remember this can be flexible as you work. From experience, I like to start with a palette, but with the expectation it will switch up as I start stitching. It may be that you need a broader palette as you can see the full embroidery start to take shape.

Step 4
Take time to test out all the stitches you have mastered. Fill in some shapes and outline others, vary your choice of

Select the colours for the wall hanging.

Use the lines as a guide to start practising the stitches you have learnt.

stitch for each shape as you go. Try to not only practise all the stitches but also experiment with the stitches you have learnt; it may be simply that you switch up stitch lengths and thicknesses as you fill a shape. As you stitch organic shapes, you will get to grips with how to stitch efficiently and you will start to develop your style before too long. Different stitches will behave differently with curves and before long you will be thinking like an embroiderer with the knowledge of how to stitch in varying situations. The purpose of this project is to force you to experiment and question your choices as you stitch. Try a mix of stitches and colours together – this is simply mark making with thread so create a wonderful wall hanging you are proud to show off.

Step 5

Your wall hanging should have a variety of geometric and organic shapes, the practice of knowing how to stitch around corners and curves will help you work out how best to tackle different shapes. At first, you may find it hard to regulate your stitches to the same sizes or it may take time to practise. You will find you speed up as the repetitive nature of embroidery will give you an eye for quick decisions on where to pull your needle through the fabric. The first mark-making hoop was simply practice – this wall hanging is about you mastering the stitches and feeling you have accomplished a piece ready for display.

Use as many different stitch types as possible and experiment with stitch lengths and thickness of thread.

Threads for Wall Hangings

- Try using one, two, three, four, five and six threads at one time. The stitches will look different with each.
- As this wall hanging is made up of many organic shapes and lines, try not to drag your thread across the back of the piece. If you have a lighter fabric you may risk seeing the thread through the front. It will be easy to finish each thread once a shape has been completed, leaving the front of your wall hanging clean with no shadows of trailing thread from the front.
- If you're feeling brave, try out a variety of thread types; it will build your knowledge of how different threads work with fabric and stitch techniques.

Finishing your wall hanging

When you are satisfied your embroidery is complete, you can finish it in one of two ways.

Option One

Cut the same size piece of fabric as the front embroidered piece. Lay the right side of your fabric, the side that your embroidery is on, to the right side of the back panel, pin them together with your pins at right angles to the edge of the fabric. You can sew up the seam allowance, use a back stitch if you don't have a sewing machine, leave a small hole at the top edge around 8cm–10cm long (this is for bagging out). Cut off the corners, being careful not to cut into your stitches – this is so when you turn it through, you have beautiful clean corners. Turn the fabric through the hole you left at the top, this can be fiddly but take your time, using something pointy but not too sharp (a knitting needle or scissors) to poke the corners out, giving a nice finish. Don't make a hole. This way all your threads and the backing of your embroidery are encased, hidden and protected. Take time to press your wall hanging. Now you need to fold the top edge towards the back; this should measure 4cm so you can stitch and fit the dowel in. Press and mark 3cm down from the top edge on the right side and pin. Sew on the front a horizontal line to catch the fold at the back. Be sure to secure the ends with back stitching on your machine at either end. See option two for details of how to add the dowel to your finished hanging.

Option Two

If you want the back of your embroidery exposed, which can be a nice feature, you need to iron the seam allowance and carefully stitch it down around the edges. Ironing flat the seam allowance and creating a clean finish on the front can be challenging. Then pin all the way around your edges with pins at right angles to the edge of your work.

Stitch all the way around with a seam allowance of around 1cm, starting and ending with a back stitch to secure the threads. When you get to the corners be sure to keep your needle in and only lift the foot to adjust your fabric positioning – this will give you a clean edging around the wall hanging. Now you need to fold the top edge towards the back, this should measure 4cm so you can stitch and fit the dowel in. Press and mark 3cm down from the top edge

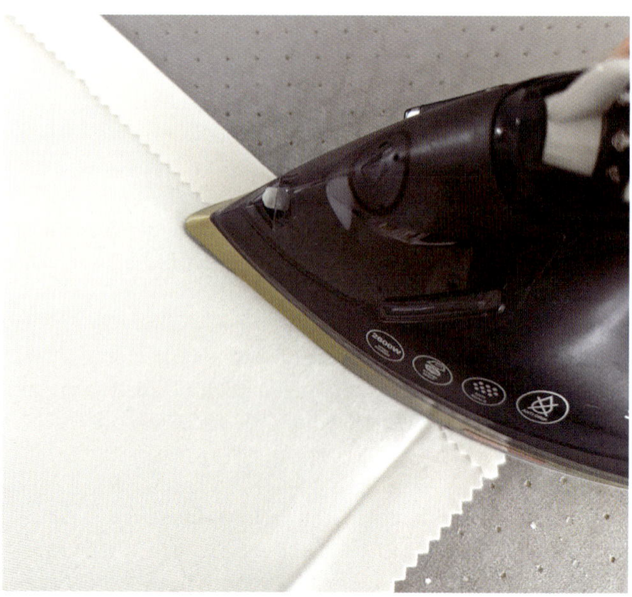

Press the edges of the back panel and front embroidery.

Place the pressed back and front on top of each other ready to be sewn.

Pin the pressed edge and sew the front embroidered panel to the back.

Insert the dowel ready to hang the piece.

Completed mark-making wall hanging in situ.

on the right side and pin. Sew a horizontal line on the front to catch the fold at the back, be sure to secure the ends with back stitching on your machine at either end.

Make holes in your dowel so you can add ribbon or string ready to hang your embroidery. Post your dowel through the tunnel you have created at the top of your fabric, add your ribbon or string and there you have it. Now to find your wall hanging a home!

Start an Embroidery Journal

When you start learning embroidery it can be a little frustrating as you get to grips with various stitches, how to move your hands and create the stitches that best suit you. Once you know what they should look like and the step-by-step rhythm for forming each stitch, it becomes easier and quicker. Your muscle memory knows what to do. A beautiful way to practise and try new stitches is by keeping an embroidery journal. You can do this in two ways:

- You could stitch fabric rectangles down the centre to create a little book. You can simply use it as a journal, stitch in it every day – you may start to stitch little pictures of things that inspired you like a tiny banana, a book or musical note. Set aside time regularly to update your stitch journal, it will help you stay organised and motivated to continue learning and creating. You can use your journal to gather inspiration from other stitchers, whether from books, online resources or social media. Above all it is a personal creative space for you to sprout and grow ideas.
- The second is simple, but just as effective for experimenting and reflecting. Use a large hoop and add daily to your little stitches and images – it may be that you include some appliqué with a mix of medium. Have fun with it!

JACOBS
MINI
CHEDDARS
ORIGINAL
BAKED WITH
CHEESE

CHAPTER 3

COPYCAT

Now you have your tools and your basic stitches are mastered, the next step is deciding what to embroider. It may be out of your comfort zone to start drawing and designing your own straight away. That aside, you still need to have the knowledge of the different ways to transfer whether from a found image, a sketch or your own design. Later we will talk about inspiration, but this chapter purely explores how to transfer your image to your fabric in different ways and how to assess what technique to use for your projects.

Now you need to get it from one place onto your fabric, ready to start stitching. Embroidering is a beautiful craft and there are so many designs available to pick up and stitch. Kits are available in abundance. This chapter is designed to encourage you to use your own found or designed images and know how to transfer your images on to fabric; it will open up many opportunities for your embroidery. The knowledge of how to transfer images will give you the opportunity to start working out who you are as an embroiderer, through the images and designs you choose, selecting ones that best reflect or express part of who you are or what you want to portray.

There are several ways to do this. You'll need to understand how each transfer process differs from the next and when to use each one. If you can transfer your image to your fabric successfully and accurately, when you come to stitch your embroidery design you will find the stitching is enjoyable. If the design has not been transferred well, you will wonder what lines you need to be following, potentially causing problems and the need to unpick part way through, which you want to avoid at all costs. The simplest and most straightforward way to transfer an image is by using a light source. If you have a design that is not too large (as you need to hold it up), or a design that is not too complex, this process is ideal. The important thing is you need to see the design lines clearly.

Transfer at a Light Source

When I prepare an image ready to transfer using a light source, I prefer to place my fabric into a size-appropriate hoop, but in reverse so that the fabric can lay flat on a surface with no space between. Some fabrics will not have a front and back and that's great, others you will need to double check. You may have a light tablet, or alternatively you can use a window. This technique will work well with lighter fabrics and even better with a more open weave.

RETRO HOOP COLLECTION PROJECT

This project is designed to kick-start your light source transfer experience. The idea is that you practise transferring a small design from paper to fabric in a small hoop. Creating a collection will give you a sense of achievement and make a great display of your achievement so far as an embroiderer. The theme for these hoops is a collection of 90s nostalgia.

You will need:

Your design, preferably a line drawing of your image
Pencil/embroidery marker or pencil
Pins
Needles
Thimbles
Cotton fabric, a light-coloured linen or board cotton
A range of embroidery hoops
A selection of threads
If you are doing a collection of hoops, it may be a good idea to transfer all images first before moving on to the next stage of the process.

Step 1
Having made a decision about how many hoops you are going to stitch for your project, it's quite aesthetically pleasing to have all of them the same size or alternatively have hoops that grow by 1in or 2in for each new hoop, for example a 3in, 5in and 7in (8cm, 13cm and 18cm) hoop collection or a 3in, 4in, 5in (8cm, 10cm, 13cm) hoop collection. Cut a generous square for each hoop, preferably with 10cm or more excess all around.

Step 2
Place fabric in all the hoops, but back to front. You would usually want the fabric tucked between the hoops with the adjustable hoop on the outside exposing the adjuster. For transferring on a light source, switch the hoops around. You're still marking your design on the right side of the fabric but for the sake of tracing from a light source, you want the fabric to be flush on the light source surface. Make sure the fabric is pulled tight so you can mark clean lines on it.

Step 3
With your fabric in your hoop, line up where you want your design to sit. Pin your design into place and leave your drawing hand free, hold up your hoop to the window with

A collection of six mini hoops filled with 90s nostalgia.

Draw up your mini designs that will fit within the hoop. You can sketch them yourself or simply find images you like and trace them.

Prep your hoops with fabric and ensure it is held taut in the hoop – this will make tracing an image and stitching much easier.

Transfer the image onto fabric using the light source method. As these are mini hoops, a window is sufficient.

Transfer all your designs before you start to stitch so you can see them as a collective before you start stitching.

the image still attached. Using a pencil or embroiderer's marker, mark up the image onto the fabric ready for embroidering.

Step 4
Take your fabric out and flip your hoops back over with the adjustable hoop now exposed and on top of the fabric. Again, make sure the fabric is firmly in the hoop ready to stitch.

Step 5
Start stitching with your chosen colours along with your chosen stitch technique. If you are stitching a collection, you may want to consider using the same stitches for each design to keep a uniform look across the hoops.

Step 6
For larger areas you could use a satin stitch for a clean block of colour and use a chain stitch for smaller areas. You may find filling in the blocks of colours and then adding thinner lines afterwards will give you a cleaner finish. This is something to try, but everyone will have a preferred order of stitching.

Step 7
Once your designs are finished, you'll need to gather the excess fabric neatly on the back of the hoop, with a running stitch all the way round. Pull it tight and secure with a knot tied to the fabric so the gathered fabric will not undo. Later in the book, we explore the ways to finish an embroidery – refer to Chapter 8 for a detailed description.

Start stitching each hoop embroidery. Make it your own – your choice of colours will make your collection of mini retro hoops unique.

Retro style mini embroideries.

Continue to use satin stitch, follow your designs and fill in the spaces.

Transfer Using Transfer Paper

Transfer paper is a brilliant tool if your fabric is too thick for a light source transfer or the fabric is too dark in colour. Different coloured embroidery transfer papers including white and yellow are available for this purpose. The transfer paper marks the fabric like a tailor's chalk; it is not permanent and will fade over time, it can also fade more quickly when over-handling the transferred areas, so be mindful once your image has been transferred. This technique is an excellent way of using black fabric. You will need to pin your paper to your fabric and line it up in the right place to avoid any movement as you start tracing over your image. An embossing tool is ideal for transferring a design, alternatively a ball-point pen will do the same job but there is a slight risk of ripping your design paper and potentially marking your embroidery fabric. Transfer tools will vary in size, which is helpful if you are transferring tiny details and delicate lines. Trace the lines with the tool pressing firmly onto a surface to ensure the chalk marks your fabric. The fabric sits under the layer of transfer paper, chalk side down, and the design sits on the top of the paper.

A helpful tip is to use a white colouring pencil or a white embroidery pencil to go over the lines once transferring is complete. The paper doesn't always give you the cleanest of lines, so enhancing them with an additional line will help you when it comes to starting your embroidery.

EMBROIDERING A PACKET PURSE

This project is a little more challenging than the previous one, as it will give you a chance to transfer a larger image and transform it into a product. We will use the embroidered piece to construct a small purse with a zip, quite challenging but achievable even with no experience. For the making stage it's best to use a machine, but if not, you can also stitch up your purse by hand. You could design your own retro-style confectionary packet, making it completely unique.

This is a fun project to get your teeth into, pardon the pun. I thought it would be a great opportunity to create a quirky purse that will wow with any outfit. What better way to do this than embroider a confectionary packet and turn it into a purse on a string. The previous project involving the light source technique was small and not too detailed, enabling you to transfer the image quickly and easily whilst holding the hoop up to the window. This transfer technique is also straightforward but due to the nature of the detail you will need to use transfer paper, an embosser and lay the fabric flat on a table. You can also leave it set up and walk away with no disturbance and with a precise and detailed finish.

The completed confectionary packet purse – a unique accessory.

Choose a packet you would be happy to wear and would be motivated to embroider. If you can, make your image larger than the original – you want your finished product to hold a few things, think of its function at this point. For this project you're not choosing colours, you're not thinking about composition and you're not thinking about adding dark and light areas – this is almost a paint-by-numbers embroidery alternative. You're going to be transferring the lines onto your fabric and then simply stitching block colours in your chosen stitch techniques. Of course, you can change the colours and vary the stitch technique, this is where your creativity comes to life, but this project is designed to focus on the transfer process so make sure you learn from the experience and grow as an embroiderer.

You will need:

- Sweet wrapper/crisp wrapper
- Plain paper and/or tracing paper
- Fabric for the purse – you will need a sturdy calico, linen or drill for this project
- Pencil/embroidery pencil marker
- Fabric marker or chalk
- Embroidery threads depending on your design
- Needle
- Embroidery hoop
- Thimble
- Transfer paper
- Masking tape
- Embossing tool/ballpoint pen
- Glue
- Lining fabric – this can be the same fabric as the front or possibly a poplin or lawn cotton; you may choose to have a tiny pattern for the inside.

Step 1
Carefully unwrap the sweet wrapper, trying not to tear it. Flatten it out as much as possible on a clean, flat surface. Smooth out any wrinkles or creases. You can then attain your image in several ways depending on what is available to you. You could scan and print or photograph and print. For all instances, you want the packet to be as flat as possible. Alternatively, if you don't have a printer, you can lay your packet flat on a surface and using tracing paper, transfer it one line at a time. It's best to trace on to paper first for better results on your fabric at the transfer paper stage.

Step 2
Now to put into practice the transfer stage. For this process we will use a transfer paper as there will be a lot of lines to trace and this is potentially too large to hold up for a length of time. Cut a generous piece of fabric as you will need to add seam allowance to your embroidery to turn it into a purse. We are trying to lower the risk of moving the image as it's transferred, so it's best on a flat surface. Ensure you have a layer of protection under your fabric, as you don't want to damage your surface as you press down. Lay the fabric out with the transfer paper chalk side facing down, ready to mark it. With each layer, tape it at the top and bottom to secure in place.

Lay the drawing or printout of the wrapper onto the top of the transfer paper again, secure it with tape top and bottom. You need to be careful when pinning as the pins through the transfer paper will mark the fabric.

Step 3
Now trace over the lines with an embosser tool or a ballpoint pen, press firmly so the marks are clear on the fabric to avoid going over the lines. When you have transferred a few lines, gently lift up your image, being careful not to shift it out of place, and check that the chalk marks can be seen on the fabric. You may need to adjust how firmly to press down with your tool. Complete the transfer in one sitting, checking you're happy with all the lines that have transferred. During the transfer process you may want to simplify your image, picking key lines could reduce the amount to embroider for the finished piece. Some lines may want defining so they are clearer for stitching.

The image transferred to fabric.

T with an embossing tool or ball point pen.

Step 4
Prepare the fabric for a purse pattern. Gently peel off the sweet wrapper from the paper, being careful not to handle the fabric too much on the front, so you're not rubbing off the chalked transfer. Carefully mark up your seam allowance around your transferred image. Give yourself a 2cm seam allowance all the way around – it's better to be generous and you can always cut it away later. Now that's all drawn up on the fabric, it's ready to hoop up and stitch.

Step 5
You may have a hoop large enough so that the complete transferred image is available to stitch with no need to move the fabric around. If not, that is fine – select an area and hoop up the fabric. If you're going to be rehooping across your fabric as you stitch, it may be wise to mark with a pen if you're confident you will cover the marks with your stitching.

Select threads according to your wrapper design, you may want to simplify the choices at this stage if you're new to embroidery. It's better that you finish a project feeling accomplished than putting it aside because you feel overwhelmed by the task you have set yourself.

Step 6
Consider what stitches you will use for the project, of course this can change but before you start the piece it's good to have an idea of what to use as a fill stitch and an outline stitch. The stitches want to be short on this piece as it is a functional product, so it's best to avoid the stitches catching or pulling during its use.

Step 7
Chain stitch or a short satin stitch are great space fillers.

Step 8
For lines and details, you could use a split stitch, back stitch or even a chain stitch like your filling stitch. Think about its function as a purse; it needs to try to limit the catches and pulls on fingers, pockets or when it goes in a bag.

Happy stitching!

Step 9
When you're satisfied you've completed your stitches, lay it flat on a surface and glue the back. Just a thin layer of PVA or even a Pritt stick will help keep all the threads on the back from fraying or trying to untie. While you leave it to dry, cut

Select the threads you will need for your project.

Start blocking out some of the larger areas. Sometimes it's best to start with the majority colour and then move to the next colour.

Fill in the spaces choosing one colour at a time.

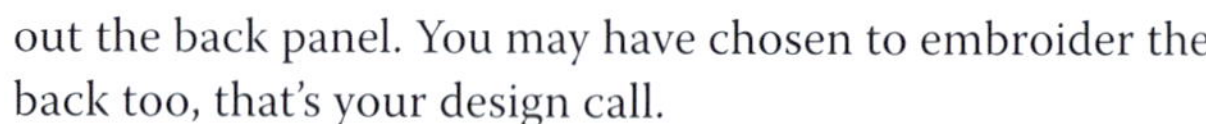

out the back panel. You may have chosen to embroider the back too, that's your design call.

Have your zip ready. Cut your embroidered piece with the seam allowance added; the back should be the same size as the front and the lining should also be the same size. You should have four pieces and a zip.

Attach the zip to the exterior fabric, place one piece of the exterior fabric right side up. Centre the zip face down along the top edge of the fabric – the key is to line it up with your embroidery so it will be flush against your zip when it's in. Place the exterior fabric right side to the right side of the fabric already attached to the zip and pin in place again with the zip at the top of your fabric.

Step 10

Sew along the edge, using a half foot on a sewing machine if you have one, catching the zipper in sewing close to the zipper teeth. Repeat for both sides of the fabric. Flip the fabric over and stitch the top edge where the zip has been attached.

Continue to stitch according to your packet design. Satin stitch may not work for all spaces; you may want to switch to lines of running stitch or chain stitch.

When it's finished, cut out the embroidery with seam allowance and stitch the zip into the top of the embroidered purse.

Step 11

Put the right sides of your outer fabric together and stitch from the right side to the left, being careful to keep your needle in and lift the foot at the corners. Next, sew up the lining from the right side around to the left paying careful attention at the corners again. You can box the corners on both the outer and lining of the purse by matching the bottom and side seams to form a triangle, measuring and marking a line perpendicular to the seam. The size will vary depending on the size of your finished piece.

Turn your embroidered fabric the right way out and press, making sure you push your corners through carefully and neatly. Next, press the top raw edge of your lining fabric over, place your lining inside your purse and carefully slip stitch the lining to the outer fabric. To make slip stitches, pull your thread through the right side of your fabric along the folded edge, stitch into the outer fabric catching just enough to hold the stitch but so it is not visible on the outside. Put the needle back into the fold and keep your stitches about 0.3cm–0.5cm apart.

Add in the zip to the top of your purse back fabric.

Step 12

Embellishment is optional and down to your discretion. You could add beads or sequins to add a little pizzazz to your finished piece, but you would do this before the make-up stage. You could even add trim to your purse which could be added into the seams during the construction stage, placing the trim sandwiched between the fabric layers. Have fun being extravagant with your creations.

Step 13

Your embroidered purse is now complete and ready to be used or gifted. Admire your handiwork and enjoy the compliments you'll receive on your unique and personalised accessory!

Gobstopper purse close-up detail.

Enjoy your creation – go show it off!

FREEHAND DRAWING

This technique is definitely not for everyone – you'll need to have some confidence in your drawing skills to use this method and get the results you want. When you have had fun sketching, you may want to scale something up or down and feel confident to do this freehand straight on to your fabric. In the past when I have taken my own still-life photos ready to embroider, drawing them up freehand gives you an extra edge of artistry but it takes confidence and practice. I tend to use it very loosely and sketchily so I can adapt and edit as I embroider. But this comes with experience and enjoying the freedom to make mistakes. This has not always worked in my favour; a few times I have not drawn up enough and lost sight of what I have been working towards. This project is a starting point for freehand drawing or a design.

Freehand Embroidered T-shirt

It may not be a technique you will find easy or choose to use, but this project will give you a chance to see if it is something

Embroidered flower meadow T-shirt showing more advanced variation ideas.

worth exploring. Using some of the stitch techniques you have recently learnt, you can quickly design and sketch out an idea ready to stitch. Drawing onto your fabric freehand can be quite exhilarating.

For this project we will be embroidering on a T-shirt, which has its own added challenges. Jersey T-shirts are a knitted fabric, therefore having an element of stretch and movement built into their structure. To stabilise the fabric, you'll need to have a woven interface support glued onto the back of your embroidery area before you start stitching. This will restrict stretching and movement in that area so that your embroidery stays in shape and is supported on the jersey. The stabiliser will also help the embroidery during the washing process.

This should give you a beginner's experience of how it feels to draw on your fabric and start stitching with a clearer idea of how the finished piece will look. If it wasn't wholly enjoyable try something else small, it may have just been the project and more experience may help. This style of image transfer is more fun over time when you gain confidence in making mistakes and knowing how to respond to problems.

The completed embroidered foliage T-shirt.

You will need:
T-shirt
Pencil/embroidery pencil or pen
Hoop
Interfacing stabiliser
Threads
Needle
Thimble

Choose your design and decide on how large it will be on your T-shirt. Consider the placement of your embroidery; you can do this by putting the garment on and checking it is positioned well. My inspiration for this freehand drawn design is plants – I find that leaves are a great way to find your hand as you can draw simple leaf shapes that are instantly recognisable once embroidered with green thread.

Step 1
Cut your fabric stabiliser. This is to give a little structure and stability with less stretch to your fabric so you can stitch it with limited movement. This will help the fabric to stay in shape and not be pulled and stretched, keeping the stitches from pulling when the garment is washed.

If you are drawing a design onto a dark fabric you can use a white colouring pencil if your embroidery pencil is a little unclear, just be sure you cover the lines with stitches as it may leave a mark. Iron your stabiliser to the inside area of where your embroidery will sit.

Step 2
Now you're ready to draw your design freehand. Make sure your T-shirt sits on a flat surface when you're drawing. It may be a challenge to get your pencil to show up – be patient and draw smaller marks rather than long lines.

Step 3
You've drawn your design and are ready to stitch; select your colours and a fine needle, so as not to pull the fabric and make unnecessary holes.

Step 4
When embroidering onto jersey, the challenge is to not pull too much on the fabric. If using stitches with loops in like the chain stitch, make them small to avoid this.

If the fabric has some movement already due to its knitted structure, it's wise to avoid stitches where there is a possibility the stitch may adjust too much.

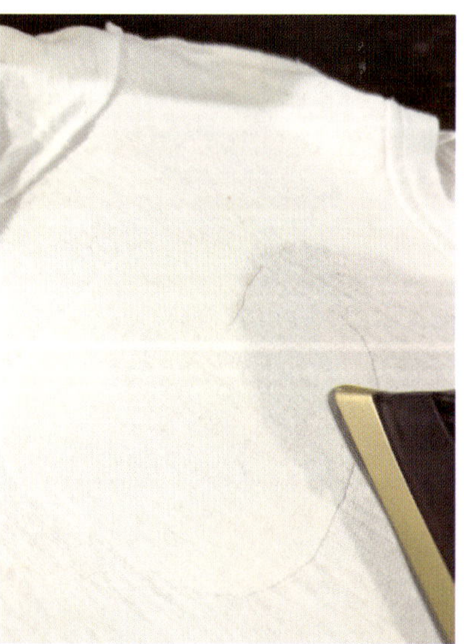

Press a patch of interfacing to the inside side of T-shirt where the design will sit.

Draw up a design with some simple leaf shapes.

Place your T-shirt with design into an embroidery hoop.

Step 5
I would suggest a short satin stitch to fill a shape or even lines of split stitch to avoid further issues with pulling against the fabric. That said, the stabiliser should help a lot, so it's always worth testing first.

Step 6
Stitch up your design ensuring you tie off and start threads with limited excess and small knots. You want to prevent the embroidery being snagged or rubbing uncomfortably against the wearer's skin.

Step 7
When you are satisfied the embroidery is complete, trim any excess thread on the back and at the knotted areas, turn the T-shirt inside out and dab a tiny amount of glue onto the knots to save any unravelling or fraying. Not too much or you will be left with a little hard lump that will irritate the skin. Leave the glue to dry, turn the top back the right way and it's ready to wear.

Start stitching on top of your design lines with simple stitches. A chain stitch makes a great stem but use small stitches on jersey to prevent pulling on the fabric.

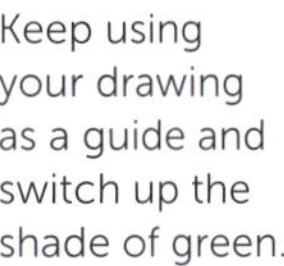

Keep using your drawing as a guide and switch up the shade of green.

If you have software which allows you to draw on a tablet or computer and you find it effective, this stick and stitch paper transfer technique is very effective. You can print your design straight on to paper and stick it to your fabric, you don't need to worry about the fabric's thickness or colour. Your design sits clearly on top of your fabric. When you have finished the embroidery, the fabric with paper attached gets soaked in water and the paper dissolves. The paper is great for accuracy and versatility of fabrics, but it may not be a very enjoyable stitching process with the paper sitting on your fabric. This is a great process when setting up kits; it takes a stage out for the stitcher. It can also be a great start for young children if the pattern is simple.

Embroidery almost complete, ready to finish off and take out of the hoop.

Transferring an image onto your fabric can be quite an intense part of the embroidery process, often it is the starting point of your design coming to fruition. From experience my preferred method is to draw my designs onto my fabric freehand. I am very confident with my drawing skills and I love the freedom drawing freehand gives me. I am often editing my image all the time, even during the embroidery stage. My style of stitching allows some freedom but my results haven't always been satisfying. I have sometimes spent too long on a piece before realising I have made a mistake by not drawing up enough of my image.

Embroidered foliage T-shirt, ready to wear.

CHAPTER 4

LEARN TO LOVE COLOUR

Using colour can be quite intimidating – where do you start? How do you select colours that go well together? How do you create a palette that creates the mood you want? All these questions over colour can be a little overwhelming, so it is important to start with the basics and over time you will learn, use your instinct more and become confident in putting colours together. The aim of this chapter is to make choosing colours exciting – using the project ideas in this part of the process should give you confidence in choosing colours and putting together beautiful and effective combinations that sing. Colours can be a signature part of how you embroider. It may be that you prefer a muted palette throughout your work, you could even choose to have a monochrome project. Colour, however, should be considered; in the same way you carefully choose a design to fit a brief, the colour selection process should be as important, selecting the right shade of blue to pair with a green is important – it's never just blue and green. The many decisions around choosing colours can be intimidating, but when you get it right it's a true delight.

One of the reasons I started creating images with thread was through my love of colour, the endless possibilities meant handmade embroidery was exciting. If you have been working through this book in chronological order, you would have had the opportunity to use a variety of colours and made some simple choices on your colour palette. It is time to understand a little more about colour, so you can make educated decisions and be confident in the choices you're making when pairing together.

In order for us to understand how to put colour together, it's important to start with the basics.

Colour theory is vital to designing so you can get the best out of your creation and send the right message to the viewer. It is a combination of art and science that helps determine what colours look good together.

Firstly, we have three primary colours: red, blue and yellow. These are the three colours that you can use to create all other colours from. If you were to mix red and blue you would have purple, blue and yellow creates green, and yellow and red make orange. Secondly, the initial colours made from combining the primary colours are purple, green and orange – these are known as the secondary colours. To create intermediate colours, otherwise known as tertiary colours, primary

Colour wheel.

Colour theory demonstration.

and secondary colours are mixed together; blue-green, blue-purple, red-orange, red-purple, yellow-orange and green-yellow. There is also a further understanding of colours known as colour properties; hue, brightness and saturation. Does it have shades, tints or tones (when small amounts of black, white and grey are added)? There is a lot of information available to help understand the science of colour, but when it comes to design and choosing colours for your embroidery you just need some basic facts so you can make an educated choice and know what works. Instinct can be the best tool you have; you can also ask other people for a second opinion, you'll soon discover if your colour palette needs adapting.

These things will become very familiar when choosing and designing with colour. It's not something to be overwhelmed by, but it is useful to know so you can make great choices.

Creating palettes of colours can be a very exciting part of the design process and bring your ideas to life. You can also generate a very different mood by changing a colour palette, even if the images you are embroidering are the same.

Below are some colour theme ideas for you to consider in your embroidery projects.

1. *Monochromatic* – you can take one colour and select several more with a variation of tints and shades. This is when black, white or grey are added. Monochromatic schemes utilise variations of a single hue by adjusting its saturation and brightness. This creates a unified and elegant aesthetic while exploring the nuances within a single colour.
2. *Analogous* – this method is about choosing colours that sit next to each other on the colour wheel. For example, reds with yellows, yellows with blues, blues with reds, even purple and greens, orange and purple. This can make for a bold palette; you may adjust the brightness of the colours within your palette to add depth and interest to your combination. Analogous colours are located next to each other on the colour wheel (for example blue, blue-green, and green). They share similar hues, creating a harmonious and cohesive palette.
3. *Complementary* – these are pairs of colours that sit opposite each other on the colour wheel. Red and green, blue and orange, yellow and purple. These are great when you're embroidering light and dark areas; the science of colour plays a great part in making your images pop when you use these complementary colours next to each other

Monochromatic.

Complementary.

Analogous.

Split complementary.

to enhance a shadow or a highlight. I use this theory a lot throughout my embroidered art and would recommend exploring it for yourself.

4. *Split complementary* – this is when you add pairs from either side of your complementary colour to give a softer contrast. For example, here are some basic split-complementary colours:
   Red + blue-green + yellow-green.
   Orange + blue-purple + blue-green.
   Red-orange + blue + green.
   Red-purple + yellow + green.
   Yellow-orange + purple + blue.
   Yellow-green + red + purple.
   Yellow + blue-purple + red-purple.
   Red + blue-purple + yellow-green.

This is enough to understand the basics of putting colours together. Sometimes you don't want a wide range of colours, it can be simply about having a saturated selection that brings all your choices together.

UNDERSTANDING HUES AND SATURATION IN COLOUR THEORY

In the vast world of colour, hues and saturation play pivotal roles in defining the richness and vibrancy of any palette. Understanding these concepts is essential for anyone working as a visual creator in any field.

The Spectrum of Hues

Hues represent the purest form of colour, often referred to as the colour wheel. This wheel encompasses all possible colours arranged in a circular format. It starts with the primary colours, red, blue and yellow, and expands into secondary and tertiary colours through mixing as mentioned earlier in this chapter.

Saturation is the Intensity of Colour

- Saturation: Also known as chroma or intensity, this refers to the purity and vividness of a colour. A fully saturated colour is vibrant and rich, while a desaturated colour appears muted or washed out.
- High saturation: Colours with high saturation are vivid and intense, appearing pure and vibrant. These colours contain little to no white, grey or black pigment, maintaining their brilliance.
- Low saturation: Desaturated colours have a reduced intensity, often resulting from the addition of white, grey or black pigments. This diminishes the vibrancy of the colour, making it appear softer or duller.

Understanding how hues and saturation interact is crucial for creating harmonious colour schemes and achieving the desired visual effects.

When you are creating an image in any medium be it abstract or realistic, understanding hues and saturation is essential for conveying emotions, creating depth and capturing attention. The manipulation of colour allows artists to evoke specific moods, emphasise focal points and engage viewers on a profound level.

Mastering the concepts of hues and saturation empowers creators to utilise colour effectively. By understanding the interaction between these elements, you can unlock endless possibilities and breathe life into your creations. You will find you will naturally gravitate to a range of colours – you may find there are already colours you prefer to choose in your fashion choices and your home decor. There is no 'wrong way' to use colour, so experiment and enjoy the process and choices available to you.

To give you some experience and practice in selecting colours, here are a few projects you can engage with and make them your own. These projects will help you experiment with colour combinations and give you confidence through experience.

CREATING A FLOWER MEADOW

This flower meadow project is an excellent way of testing and trying out colours together. There's not too many stitches at one time in the same colour, so the pace at which you need to choose your colours will help you to be decisive in your selections and give you the opportunity to make lots of combinations in quick succession. This flower piece is inspired by a huge embroidery I completed a few years ago. Lost Love was a very large wall hanging of tiny flowers embroidered onto a vintage tablecloth. This embroidery was truly a labour of love; it took many more months than planned and was an expression of the world being turned upside down by the effects of the pandemic in 2020. Lost Love represents all the lost lives we experienced through the pandemic, it speaks of the beauty of life itself, but also of its vulnerable nature that can be gone in an instant.

This project explores a small example of this. It is not designed to be a full exploration of colour, you'll be considering your colour palette and potentially identifying a style of colouring that you may carry on to use throughout your embroidery journey. Is your palette muted, bold, gentle, exotic? What do your choices say about your style and you?

Flower meadow.

You will need:
7in (18cm) hoop
Needles
Snips
Fabric, preferably light coloured
Paper
Pen
Pencil/embroidery pencil
Thread in abundance – this is your excuse to start building your thread collection
Thimble

You have a few options when it comes to preparing your fabric and thinking about your flower embroidery. You could draw flowers straight on to your fabric so you can see where each flower will sit and position them with space around each, checking your composition within the hoop before you start stitching. Alternatively, you can draw around your hoop on paper and draw up your design before you transfer your composition. If you're feeling confident you can stitch one flower at a time and consider the position of the next on the completion of a flower. No way is wrong and sometimes it's a trial-and-error situation.

For this chapter, you will need to use most of the stitches that you learnt earlier in the book. The difference will be that you'll need to think about how the stitches form a flower shape; some stitches will be the same but the position and composition will vary depending on what the flowers look like. The purpose of this project is to practise selecting colours and pairing them together – it may be that you have three or four colours per flower and this makes for great practice, moving on from one choice to another. Like all the projects in this book, use the ideas to inspire and propel your creativity.

For this project you will need to know:

- Satin stitch
- French knots
- Split stitch
- Lazy daisy
- Blanket stitch

If you want to draw up your whole design prior to stitching, read through the step-by-step guide so you can see what is required before you start; this way you draw up each flower on your design according to the guidance for this project. If you're confident about getting started, you will be drawing up one flower at a time and stitching according to the step-by-step guide.

Start your miniature rose with five spokes coming from the centre of your circle.

Step 1

Hoop up your fabric making sure it's as tight as a drum. This will give you successful stitches as you pull thread in and out of the fabric. When you're happy with your design, transfer your image using a light source as described, or draw straight onto the fabric. Select around 15–18 colours, picking a few from each colour variety; reds, yellows, blues, purples, greens and oranges.

This project will be broken down into a variety of flowers. Each step will be a new flower; you can use as many or as few colours per flower as you want.

Step 2

The first flower will be a miniature rose. Select your first colour and thread your needle. You're going to need to draw a base for your stitches as a guide. Draw a small circle, around the size of a five-pence piece, with five roughly equally spaced lines coming out from the centre to the outside circle line.

Step 3

Stitch over each line with your thread. Choose a starting point, slide your needle under one of your stitched lines and then over the next. Keep doing this in a circle, weaving in and out of your stitched lines until you reach the edge. To finish, pull your needle to the back and tie off securely before snipping the excess.

Continue weaving your needle and thread over and under the spokes until the rose is complete.

Step 4

You can vary this by having a bigger circle and adding more lines out from the centre. This pattern works on an odd number of lines coming from the centre, so if you're doing a bigger circle you could add more central lines, but it should be either seven or nine. To finish the flower, add a simple stem with split stitch or running stitch.

Step 5

The lazy daisy stitch is so incredibly satisfying, it's almost a deconstructed chain stitch so you will have a foundation on which to stitch the second flower. Draw yourself a simple flower, start in the middle and draw around eight petals from the centre to complete your circle, each petal should be between 0.5cm and 1cm in length. Select a new colour, take two or three strands from your skein, thread up the needle and knot the end of your thread. Pull your needle through the centre of your flower and straight back in through the same hole, but only pulling the thread halfway through. You should have a loop. If you keep pulling the stitch will disappear; you need to interrupt the loop with thread so at the top of the petal shape drawn on your fabric, bring the needle back through to the right side approximately 0.5cm–1cm from the centre, keeping the loop from disappearing. As you pull the thread through, the loop will be held by your new stitch. Bring your needle to the other side of the loop and back into the fabric just the other side of the loop, pull tight – there you have your first petal stitch.

Rose flower completed, add a tiny stem and leaves to finish.

Step 6

Repeat the process until your petals complete the circle. Finish the flower by stitching a French knot at the centre in a different colour and add a stem and some satin-stitched leaves. To vary this, you may choose to do two or three layers or change the size and colour of the petals.

Step 7

Draw your third flower onto your hoop. It's simple in its form but may take a while to complete. Draw two vertical lines crossing over each other about 0.5cm from the bottom of your line. Make each line around 2cm–3cm long. Then using the lines as a guide, create French knots as described in Chapter 2. First in one colour, then in a shade lighter or darker of the same colour.

Step 8

Repeat the French knots until the lines are surrounded by them. You can make the knot larger or smaller by increasing or decreasing the amount of times you wrap the thread around the needle. Add long green leaves and stems by using a running stitch or stem stitch.

Lazy daisy stitch, which is like a chain stitch broken down one stitch at a time.

Continue the lazy daisy stitch to complete the flower. You can also finish the flower with a French knot at the centre.

Finish the flower by adding French knots along the stem. Vary the shades of purple and add leaves in green to finish.

Once you have drawn a line as your stem, start stitching French knots along the line.

Step 9

Similar to a French knot, the fourth flower involves a bullion knot. Instead of wrapping your thread around your needle once or twice, you do this five times. Start as you would for all the other flowers by drawing a template onto your fabric where you want your flower to sit. For this one you'll need six lines, roughly evenly spaced, coming out from the centre. The lines and number of times you wrap thread around the needle will vary if you want different sizes. Start with lines that are around 0.7cm from the centre of your flower.

Step 10

Cover all the lines with the bullion knot one at a time, working your way around the flower one petal at a time. Add a stem and leaves if you want at this point. Bring the needle and thread up from the back to the front of your fabric and through the centre of your flower template. Pull the thread all the way through, keeping your needle close to the entry point, wrap the thread around the needle five times, then making sure that all the stitches stay on the needle push back through the fabric at the end of one of your drawn lines. As you do this, the stitches may need a little help off the needle as the thread goes back through the fabric. You should be left with a beautiful bullion petal.

Step 11
Carry on a repeat for the rest of the lines on your template. You can vary this by putting two layers of petals on top of each other, or make the template circle bigger and each petal longer, allowing more space to stitch more petals.

Step 12
For the fifth flower you can draw a half flower with rounded petals or a larger flower – all the flowers so far have been quite delicate so you can be bold with this one.

The first petal in the bullion flower.

Start the next petal with the same process as the first, then move on to the next until the flower is complete.

Completed bullion flowers.

Start your petal with the first blanket stitch. You may need to draw a circle as a guide before you start your flower.

Separate two or three strands of embroidery floss from the skein. Embroidery floss is often made up of multiple strands twisted together for a standard blanket stitch. Thread your needle and knot the end with a single or a double knot to secure the thread. To start your blanket stitch petals, bring your needle up through the fabric from the back to the front at the starting point of your flower's outline. Insert the needle back into the fabric slightly to the right or left of the starting point, about 0.6cm away. Pull the thread through, leaving a small loop. Bring the needle back up through the fabric at a point along the outline of the flower, about 0.6cm away from the first stitch. Make sure the needle passes through the loop created by the previous stitch. Pull the thread tight to create the first of the blanket stitches. This should create a diagonal line along the edge of your fabric.

Step 13

Repeat the process, making evenly spaced stitches along the entire outline of the flower. Each stitch should be the same length and angle, creating a uniform appearance. As you work your way around the flower, adjust the angle of your stitches to follow the curves of the outline. To create petals, you can vary the length and spacing of your stitches. For example, you might make longer stitches along the outer edge of the petal and shorter stitches toward the centre. Experiment with different stitch lengths and angles to achieve the desired petal shape and texture.

Once you've completed the outline of the flower, tie off the thread on the back of the fabric with a knot. Trim any excess thread. If you desire, you can add additional details to your flower, such as French knots for the centre or additional embroidery stitches for leaves or stems. Embroidering a blanket stitch flower requires patience and practice, but with time, you'll master the technique and be able to create beautiful embroidered flowers and designs.

Continue stitching petals with approximately four or five blanket stitches in each petal, until the flower is complete.

Step 14

The sixth flower should resemble a tulip. The easiest way to start is by drawing a long stem with two long leaves either side. At the tip of the stem, draw three lines about 1cm long coming out of the top, one down the centre and two at a slight angle away from each other. You'll need two colours for each flower. At the top of your stem choose a colour to go over the three lines and simply stitch one stitch per line. Using a new colour, bring the needle up through the fabric at the point where the flower petals meet the stem, take it back through at the entry point leaving a loop, similar to making a lazy daisy petal, then bring the needle back to the front of the fabric at the top of the petal and fasten the loop by stitching just over the thread. Repeat this for the other two petals on the flower to create your tulip. It's a very simple flower to embroider, there are also options to make it interesting by adding extra colours and varying the sizes.

Step 15

Draw up your own flower design – you can draw in as few as three petals for a half-open flower or lots of skinny petals. This method for creating a flower is extremely versatile. Even on this small project, you can experiment with this technique many times. Fill the flower with a simple satin stitch, using short or long stitches.

Finished tulip flower.

Now you have had a chance to put the understanding of colour theory into practice on a small scale, you should be able to see how it plays out in your design. The challenge is to move onto something a little more complex where considering the colours will have a larger impact on the overall look of your finished piece.

You have experimented and tested seven flower ideas, but the techniques these flowers have taught you have provided the potential to explore further and create some extremely interesting creations. Even if you use these basics and change up the sizes and colours, you will find you have a plethora of beautiful flowers. Keep creating and pairing colours together. This project should give you space to put colours together and create a stunning flower meadow. If you enjoy the process, switch up to a larger hoop with an array of flowers more varied than before.

Now you have all the stitches and flower variations to create a flower meadow hoop that is unique.

Lost Love close-up detail.

Flower meadow with hand-painted bamboo hoop.

An array of flowers in pinks.

EYE EMBROIDERY

The human face is a captivating subject for artists due to its versatility and expressiveness. Each feature, from the eyes to the mouth, offers a wide range of emotions and nuances that artists can manipulate to convey their unique style. Moreover, because facial features are instantly recognisable and deeply ingrained in our perception, they serve as a powerful tool for visual communication in art. Artists can play with proportions, angles and details to evoke different moods, personalities and narratives, making the human face a brilliant canvas for their creativity. For this next project we will be using eyes as our subject. It's a great way of putting colour theory to the test on a more challenging level than the flower hoop project.

Finding the Best Image

Firstly, let's talk about selecting your eye image. We will be embroidering in a 7in (18cm) hoop so you will need to look for an image where the eye is around 10cm. Our embroidered area will expand further than this, but it will make for a good composition within the hoop to give space around the embroidery. Start researching and sourcing eye images, through magazines, internet printouts or even your own sketches. Once you start looking at images you may feel overwhelmed by the options; the best way to select is to pick around five you like and then start comparing them to each other, eliminating the ones with less impactful compositions until you're left with one you are happy to use as a pattern to stitch from.

Detailed study of an eye in blue and yellow.

You will need:
An image of an eye
Pencil/embroidery pencil
Scissors
Snips
Needles
Coloured thread
Thimble
7in (18cm) hoop
Cotton, black or white

Step 1
For this project, using transfer paper is going to be the most efficient way of getting your image onto fabric, whether it's a sketch, a magazine cutting or a printout. Using transfer paper for black or white fabric will give all the lines you need ready to stitch without hassle. Layer up your fabric, transfer paper face down on your fabric with your image sitting on top. Tape all the layers one at a time to your surface so nothing can move. Using a ballpoint pen or embossing tool, trace your image to transfer to the fabric.

Step 2
Now your images are on your fabric, check over the lines making sure you're happy that they are as clear as they need to be. If some are faint go over them with an embroidery pencil or a lead pencil. If you're guessing lines during the stitching process you may have to correct or unpick, which should be avoided if possible. Now you're ready to select your colours; based on the knowledge of colour theory you have learnt earlier in the chapter, you can put into practice some ways of selecting colours. An easy way to start is by choosing analogous colours and then bringing in one or two complementary shades to enhance shadow areas. I find it's always important to have white, and to take a few shades between the white and your brightest colour.

Step 3
You're ready to start stitching – this is where you can have fun. With all the mark-making skills you have learnt and

explored, you can apply this with the colour palette and make your eye study come alive. Take a moment to pause and see where the darkest and lightest areas sit on your image, consider the palette that you have selected and have a clear idea what colours will represent the different tones. You want to create depth to your embroidery; thinking about colour before you start stitching will have the potential to flatten or lift your embroidered piece.

Step 4
As you start to put stitch to fabric, remember to shape your stitches according to your image, look at where the curves are on the cheek bone or around the eyebrow, try to create this shadow not only through your use of colours but also the directions you take the stitches in.

Start stitching with the mid blue shades you have previously selected.

Step 5
Consider how far apart your stitches are from each other; the closer they are there will be an illusion of shadow or if you space them out further or stitch tiny details there will be less intensity of colour, creating the appearance of a lighter area. Start with your darkest shade and get all your shadows and dark areas in.

Start stitching a lilac or light purple into your embroidery, gradually blending into the blue with small stitches.

Step 6
At this point you will have to trust the process – it will take time to have that experience of knowing you're on the right track, I still often wobble about halfway through any piece! Start adding your mid tones, blending as you go; you never want a harsh line of colour change unless it's in your design, and thinner threads will help with this. Take time to add stitches, not too large as you'll want a smooth blend of colours.

Step 7
Your study of an eye embroidery should be taking shape and you will start to see where you're heading. You should have your darkest and mid colours down, so now for the lighter ones. I like to leave my white highlights until last as it's actually very rewarding to put them in and see your work come to life. With your lightest tones, blend them well and consider carefully where they go – less is more with the lighter shades. Too much and your embroidered eye will lose

Adding a dark purple and a deeper yellow/ orange thread to the shadow will enhance the darker shadowed areas.

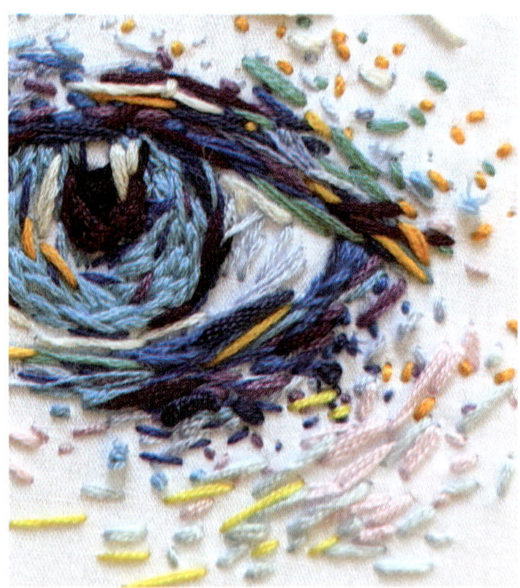

Eye study detail.

definition, too little and the contrast won't be enough. You'll be surprised how few stitches will make a big difference.

Step 8
Take a step back and check you're happy so far, you may need to add an extra shade of mid tone for blending purposes. When you're satisfied you have most of your range of tones down on the canvas it's time to introduce the complementary colours. You will very quickly see the vital role they play in bringing your embroidery to life. You will only need a small amount and it may just be a few stitches around your embroidery. It's complementary because it is an opposite colour; on your shadows take your complementary colours and add some extra depth to the areas that are dark and lighter, it makes most sense to place the colours along an edge to create a defined shadow or in the highlighted area, as this will make your creation pop. Keep taking a step away and coming back to your embroidered piece; sometimes you can become too familiar while stitching a piece and lose sight of what it needs. Take a moment away, make a cup of tea, you may instantly see what it needs when you return. Don't forget to add your highlights right at the end – you want to leave this until last as I often find stitching across other stitches, the contrast with your white thread has a great effect and helps the highlights to appear even brighter.

Well done, you should be proud of yourself for creating a unique embroidery from start to finish. This project should have given you confidence in choosing colours and the ability to make choices with your stitch direction that will make your piece wow the viewer. Be inspired and keep moving forward with using colour and creating stunning embroidery.

Now all the knowledge you've gained so far has been put into action, transferring your image onto fabric was a bridge from imagination to realisation, the eye project should have given you the confidence you need to propel yourself forward in transferring designs, applying colour theory and utilising your stitches. The next challenge is to take this knowledge, and practise driving yourself forward into another project. The human face, as mentioned earlier, is an excellent visual for artists to study and interpret. From the gentle curves of a smile to the sparkle in the eyes, use each stitch like a brushstroke and create a full portrait in thread, experimenting using limited lines and then push to larger, more intense pieces with attention to detail and a wider palette of colours. Select a portrait you are inspired to stitch; it may be someone dear to you or that inspires you. Decide on how you're going to approach your portrait; is it going to be a realistic stitch project or will you be switching colours and abstracting your image for stitching? Challenge yourself, push boundaries and have fun with faces!

Eye study in blue and yellow.

Grapefruit on yellow gingham.

ML K CHOC

CHAPTER 5

CAPTURE THE LIGHT

As an artist, it has taken many years to find my style, discover the ways I love to work and determine which parts of the creative process to embrace or avoid. As you practise and uncover your own style, you will quickly identify the aspects you enjoy and learn strategies to bypass the less pleasurable parts. One of my strengths, as you may have noticed in my work, is playing with the contrast of light and dark. As an embroidery artist, it has been a journey of experiments to best showcase light and shadow within my pieces. Using thread makes this process even more challenging, as there are no tools to smudge or sharpen the details that define light and dark areas. The medium is not versatile; it is through the choice of colours and mark making that definition is achieved.

When I envision an image to recreate in thread, the best place to start is with the initial image itself. This could be a found image, which is perfectly fine, especially if you are not accustomed to composing an image from scratch. A found image provides a great starting point. Begin by selecting an image to transfer, choose your fabric, hoop up and start stitching.

This chapter will provide you with tips on how to take a photo and edit it to serve as a great springboard as you begin your embroidery process with a focus on light. In the previous chapters, we learned how to make marks and transfer an image. By now, you have the basic skills and enough practice to embark on a new challenge. Like all these steps, becoming a bolder and more confident stitcher requires practice. Capturing light in your embroidery will move you beyond simple mark-making and colour-by-number techniques, steering you towards creating lifelike images and presenting your embroidery in a realistic manner.

To help you understand how to best capture light and stitch a piece that not only looks realistic but also excites an audience, we will undertake a few small projects. Projects one and two are similar in nature; what better way to capture light than by using subjects like fruit and vegetables? These are excellent for capturing light without the complications of numerous colours. Take a tomato, for instance. The primary colour is red, and when capturing it in thread, you will focus on the shades of red to best display the changes of light across the piece. The chapter on colour will be very helpful, and you can use it to your advantage to achieve the best results in your finished embroidery.

Once you have mastered capturing light through editing, you will be able to look at an image and translate it into stitches on your canvas, bringing your embroidery to life.

CHILLIES PATCH

The first project is small and relatively quick to complete. This will give you the initial steps in observing light and capturing it in a few stitches, which will start to bring your mark-making and colour selection skills together.

This first project is a step-by-step guide to creating fruit/veg patches for customising clothing. Creating a patch gives you versatility. All your hard work can be recycled when your clothing is worn out – simply unpick it and restitch it to a new item. You can also use a patch to place on items that are a little tricky to stitch straight onto.

Nothing says fun more than a pair of chillies on an item of clothing. The best way to capture your chillies takes a little time but you don't need expensive equipment. I love to draw, so quite often this results in taking a photograph, drawing from the photo and using felt pens to simplify the light and dark areas ready to translate to stitch. Red chillies are a great way to start, as red shows a lovely contrast of light and shadow.

Chillies patches.

Prep for Your Photo

Set up a clear space, preferably with a sheet of clean white paper and set your chillies on it with plenty of space around them. Your focus is the chillies, so clear anything else from the background. Set this space up preferably with some natural light that will give you the best results. Sometimes it will help to have a lamp giving extra light, so you can move it as you try to capture the best image.

Taking Photos

- Golden hours: Shoot during the golden hours (shortly after sunrise or before sunset) for soft, warm light.
- Shadow play: Embrace shadows as part of the composition for a dramatic effect.
- Background check: Always check the background for distractions before taking the shot.

By following these steps, you can capture well-lit, beautifully composed photos of objects and still life scenes without the need for specialised equipment. Give yourself a clean space and a clean surface. If you're going to get serious with taking your own photos I would suggest investing in a piece of large white foam board. This is a great tool to have – it will give you photos that will be easy to work with. Whether you're setting up a large still life or a simple object, composition is so important to the visual takeaway. For the purpose of this chapter, our focus is on capturing light so you can translate it with stitches and create a beautiful embroidery that comes alive. You can create a brighter highlight or a darker shadow shining a lamp on an area; it depends what you're aiming to achieve but you want a great contrast between the lightest and darkest areas on your chillies. When you have taken your photo, adjust the size if you need to and print off the image ready for transfer.

Taking the Photo

Taking a great photo of an object or still life without specialist equipment involves careful consideration of lighting, composition and camera settings. Here's a step-by-step guide to help you achieve the best results:

Step 1
Choose the right location; look for somewhere with abundant natural light. A spot near a large window is ideal. Avoid direct sunlight as it can create harsh shadows and overly bright highlights. Opt for indirect or diffused light.

Step 2
Set up your scene, choosing a clean, uncluttered background that contrasts well with your subject. Place your object on a flat, stable surface like a table or counter. Position your object or still life arrangement thoughtfully. Consider balance, symmetry and the rule of thirds (*see* page 89).

Capturing light for an image. For a contrast in light and dark when taking a photo, place the object in full light, adjust the object for best results (yellow arrow indicates light). The brighter the light, the stronger the shadow (blue arrows).

Step 3
If the light is too harsh, diffuse it using a white sheet, curtain or even a piece of paper to soften shadows. Use a white or silver surface, like a piece of cardboard covered in aluminium foil, to reflect light onto your subject and fill in shadows.

Step 4
Compose your shot; experiment with different angles and perspectives. Shoot from above, at eye level or at a slight angle to find the most flattering view. Use the rule of thirds to place your subject off-centre for a more dynamic composition. Imagine a grid over your viewfinder and place key elements along these lines.

Step 5
Adjust camera settings, ensuring your subject is in sharp focus. Most smartphones and cameras have touch-to-focus features. Adjust the exposure to ensure your photo isn't too dark or too bright. On smartphones, tap on the subject and slide the exposure indicator up or down. Ensure the colours are accurate by adjusting the white balance setting if your camera or phone allows it. If you can't do this at the point of taking the photo, it should be possible during the editing process.

Step 6
Steady your camera to avoid blurry photos. Use a tripod if available or rest your camera on a stable surface. Take multiple shots capturing several photos from different angles and with slight variations in lighting and exposure.

Step 7
Use a photo editing app to make basic adjustments; you should be able to adjust brightness, contrast and saturation. Crop the image to enhance composition and straighten any tilted lines. Enhance details by sharpening the image slightly; this will ensure it looks crisp.

Step 8
Print out the image; make sure you have made it a good size for your patch. If you are following the project exactly, you're looking for it to fit nicely towards the back of your canvas shoe. If you're not happy, adjust and reprint.

You can choose to find an image, draw from life or take your own photo to capture the best light for your patches.

Transfer your image using your preferred method. As it's a small embroidery, the light source transfer is a good option.

You can alternatively draw up your image. This is a way that I like to make my embroideries even more unique, I find the process of drawing adds an extra depth to my work.

Transfer your image on to your chosen fabric. If your canvas shoe is light in colour transfer your image to a white fabric, or a black if your canvas shoe is a darker colour. I suggest you use the transfer paper method of transferring your image, as there may be a level of detail for capturing the light that you'll want to mark down. This may potentially be easier than a light source transfer. You will be transferring two of the same image for your shoe patches. You want them to be the same so it's a good idea to have two hoops ready with fabric so you can transfer the images one after the other before stitching.

Step 9

Before you transfer the chillies onto fabric, mark out the areas where you have varying shadows and light, then transfer this onto paper first so that the image you're copying onto your fabric is simplified and you can see exactly where you plan to add highlights and shadows. You'll need to plan before you start stitching where your darker shades and mid tones are on your image. When you have transferred the image onto the fabric it will be a series of defined contour lines – the idea is that these are a guide for blending when you begin to stitch, to help bring your chillies patch to life. Now transfer onto fabric.

Step 10

Select the colours according to the image. Red is a great colour to use to create your patches and capture light, even with one colour the mid tones and lighter tones are defined, making for an effective finished embroidery. You may find you choose some pinks and peach tones which will help capture the light and dark contrast in your chillies patch. Initially select two each of dark, mid and light tones – these can be added to if you feel it is needed for blending, but this is a good starting point.

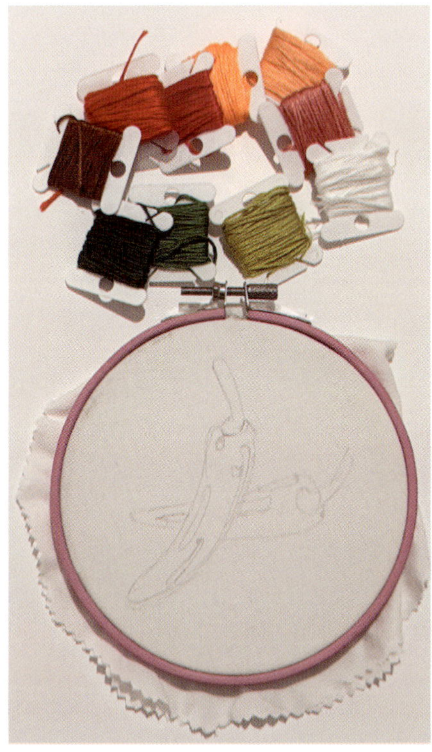
Select the colours in preparation for your embroidery. You'll need mid tones along with some very dark and very light.

Add the mid shades of reds, these may be more pinky in colour. Look carefully and keep referring to your original image.

Step 11
At the beginning of the book, you learnt some basic stitches. This is to broaden your knowledge of embroidery and help in your various projects. If you look closely at my embroidered pieces, you will see that I have mostly used a version of satin stitch, sometimes in an orderly fashion and at others you can see I'm changing direction or adding a new colour along with the change of direction. This is part of the style that I have formed over the years; there is an element of this that can't be taught, it's intuitive to me, as an artist. You can experiment with this style and of course, I hope that you create a new style that best fits you.

Do use satin stitch with the freedom to make it your own. For this patch project remember you are capturing light, you have your areas of shadows and highlights marked on your fabric, you have your colours and now it's time to stitch.

Step 12
Choose a stitch you prefer and start filling the areas. Use no more than three strands at a time for this project. When it comes to blending colours, you want the line between colours to be gradual and as soft as you can make it. Small amounts of colour interspersed will help with blending colours and creating an ombre effect.

Step 13
When you're satisfied the chillies are ready for finishing and applying to the shoes, you should have two that look alike, unless you have chosen not to.

Step 14
Turn over your embroidered hoops and apply a thin layer of glue – PVA or simply a glue stick – across the back of your embroideries. Extend the glued area to about 0.5cm beyond your stitching and then leave to dry, preferably overnight.

Start adding the orange shades or lighter reds to the embroidery. Try to add them to both embroideries at the same time if you're aiming to have a pair of patches.

Now both embroideries are ready to be prepared and turned into patches.

Finish adding all the lightest green areas. It may only be a few stitches to help the embroidery come to life.

Add a thin layer of glue to seal the back of the embroidery. Let it dry – this may take 24 hours depending on the glue.

Step 15
When the glue is dry, it may remain slightly tacky, cut out each embroidery around 0.5cm away from the edge of the design. Carefully take the time to fold back the fabric edges and they should stick a little to the back of the embroidery. Using a needle and thread, two strands, carefully slip stitch around the edge of the embroidery patch ensuring you catch all the edges tucked to the back. This will take longer than you think but it's worth doing for a tidy finish.

Step 16
Finally you can attach the patch to the canvas shoes. Use a pin at the top and bottom of the patch to hold it in place. Using a needle and thread, you can manipulate the edges to keep them tucked in as you stitch. Lots of small stab stitches are better than long, visible stitches. When you're finishing a project it's very tempting to rush, but take your time to apply the patches well to show off your hard work. All the time spent on your embroidery will be wasted if they are badly sewed on.

Ta da – done! Now show them off.

Once the glue has dried, cut around the chillies with a small seam allowance.

Detail of chillies patches.

THE IMPORTANCE OF COMPOSITION IN ART

Composition is just as important as light and its effect on an image. A creative composition can be the difference between drawing your audience in or disengaging them. The next section will give you some key elements to think about when constructing a still life or composing an image.

Understanding composition is key to creating a successful piece of art. Composition in art refers to the arrangement of visual elements within a piece. This involves considering how objects are positioned on the canvas to create a harmonious and engaging artwork. A well-composed piece draws the viewer's eye through the artwork, creating a sense of balance and guiding attention to the focal points.

The Key Elements of Composition

Balance
Balance refers to the distribution of visual weight within the artwork. There are two main types:

- Symmetrical balance is when objects are evenly distributed on either side of the central axis. This creates a sense of stability and order.

- Asymmetrical balance is when different elements have varying visual weights but are arranged in a way that still feels balanced. This often results in a more dynamic and interesting composition.

Focal Points

Focal points are areas of interest that attract the viewer's eye. These can be created using:

- Contrast, either in the use of differences in colours, light or texture which can make certain areas stand out.
- Placement and positioning of objects can be important. Placing something in an area of prominence such as the intersection points in the rule of thirds.
- Adding more detail to certain parts and areas of the artwork can draw the viewer's attention.

Rule of Thirds

The rule of thirds involves dividing the canvas into a 3×3 grid, creating nine equal parts. Key elements should be placed along these lines or at their intersections. This technique helps in creating more dynamic and engaging compositions compared to simply centring subjects.

Leading Lines

Leading lines are lines within the artwork that guide the viewer's eye towards the focal points. These can be actual lines or implied lines created by the arrangement of objects. An example of this could be the positioning of a road, a river or the gaze direction of a figure within the artwork.

Depth and Perspective

Creating a sense of depth adds realism and interest to a composition. This can be achieved in several ways including linear perspective and using vanishing points to create the illusion of depth. Overlapping objects by placing one object in front of another can create a sense of space. Vary the size of objects to give the illusion of depth, larger in the foreground and smaller in the background.

CONSIDERATIONS FOR YOUR CANVAS

There are always many things to consider when creating an image, which can at first be overwhelming. As you experiment and practise more it will become more intuitive over time.

Size and Shape

The size and shape of your canvas influences the composition significantly. A larger canvas offers more space for complex compositions, while smaller canvases may require simpler arrangements. The shape (square, rectangle and so on) can also affect how elements are perceived.

Decide whether your canvas will be oriented vertically (portrait) or horizontally (landscape). This choice can affect the mood and focus of your composition. For instance, a horizontal orientation might suit landscapes, while a vertical orientation might emphasise height and elegance in portraits.

Consider the negative space, the area around and between objects. Negative space can provide breathing room for the viewer's eye and help to emphasise the main subjects. Avoid cluttering the canvas; sometimes it's important to allow some margins around the edges to frame your composition.

Placing the main subject in the centre can create a strong focal point but might also result in a static composition. Central placement works well for symmetrical designs or when the subject is intended to be the dominant element. Alternatively, positioning the subject off-centre, especially along the lines of the rule of thirds, creates a more dynamic and engaging composition. This placement often results in a more natural and pleasing visual flow. You may have heard of the terms foreground, middle ground and background, in other words the closest elements, the elements between the back and the front and the elements positioned furthest away. Using these three planes can add depth and context to a composition.

By understanding and applying these principles of composition, as an artist you too can create visually compelling and harmonious works that captivate viewers and convey your intended message effectively.

FRUIT HOOPS

This project will give you the opportunity to put into practice the knowledge of capturing light and how to make a great composition. This is the beginning of exploring still life in embroidery; start small with the aim that you are working towards a larger project when composition will be the focal point. This fruit hoop project takes you step by step through the process of embroidering a lemon, or another fruit if you choose to take the steps and make them your own.

Fruit hoops. Using complementary colours to enhance the light and shaded areas of embroideries.

You will need:

8in (20cm) embroidery hoop
Needles
Thimble
Pencil/embroidery pencil
Scissors/snips
Fabric – a cotton linen is quite a lovely fabric to embroider on. Choose a light colour.
(With experience you will find the fabrics you prefer to stitch on.)
Threads

Your preferred method of transfer is either a photo with transfer paper, a light source and tools or if you're confident, you can draw your still life straight onto fabric with a freehand technique.

At this point you want to find the dominant colour. We will mostly be working in a monochromatic way, so select the same colour with tints and shades, lighter and darker than your main colour. The more you have the more you can blend, but three lighter and three darker will be a great start for this project. You will also need some complementary colours to help your fruit pop off the canvas. So if you're going to be stitching a lemon, you will have mostly yellows with a few blues and peachy/light pinks. You will also need a white thread.

Step 1

Compose the image you're hoping to translate into embroidery. Consider all that has been talked about previously in this chapter. Choose a fruit or vegetable. How are you capturing light? Have you composed your image well, is it interesting for the viewer? Cutting the fruit in half and arranging it will give a dynamic composition for this project. Consider it for your own embroidery. Even if you are planning on drawing your fruit freehand onto your fabric, take a photo as this is the best way to see if the composition is going to work well on your canvas. From experience even if I am not transferring an image using a paper or light source, I nearly always need to adjust and edit the photo of my embroidery to be the best it can be. One of the great things about embroidering fruit is its simplicity; you're not having to look at too many details and it's instantly recognisable once the simple shape has colour. It's easy for the viewer to understand what they are looking at.

Step 2
Transfer your image onto your chosen fabric and then place the fabric firmly in the hoop. It should be held taut and sound drum-like when tapped, so that you can stitch all parts of your image without repositioning the fabric during the embroidery process.

Step 3
At this point take a little look at the fruit you will be stitching. Mark your fabric where you can see the colour get darker and lighter, draw this onto the fabric image – it will then look like it has contour lines. With experience you may not choose to draw these lines in, but as we start it's a great

At this point, if you are confident you will cover the marks in stitches you may want to go over them in pen to ensure you can see the markings.

Once you have drawn up your lemon and marked out areas, you'll need to think about your thread colours.

way to concentrate on blending colours. Take a bit of time to choose what colours are going into the various spaces you have marked out.

You are not tied to anything; if you want to change it, add an extra shade. This is part of the process. Critiquing your work as you stitch is a great way to learn and improve.

Step 4
Line up your colours, with your main colour in the middle and the lighter and darker shades either side. This will help you keep track of the colours you're using for lighter and darker areas on the embroidery.

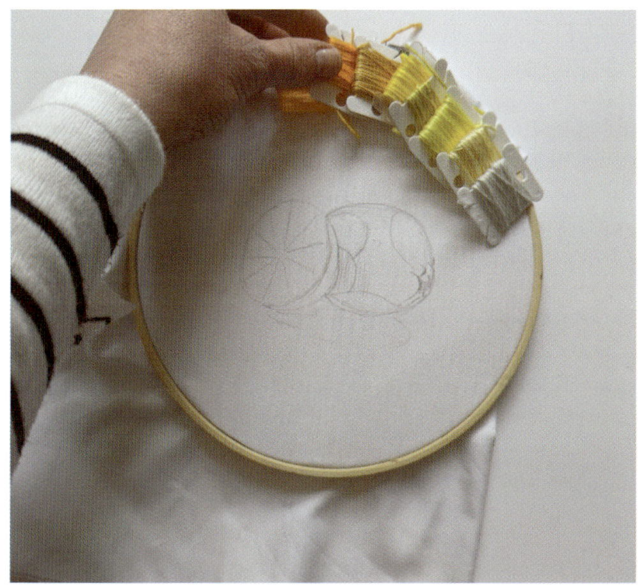

Select the shades of yellow for your embroidery. A range of mid tones is essential, then you'll need a range of darker and lighter shades. This can vary depending on how you want your finished piece to look.

Add in the mid yellow shades to start getting the majority of the yellow in place on the lemon.

Step 5

For this project, you will mostly use a satin stitch with a few French knots to add texture and a concentration of detail. Choose the area on your fruit where your main colour sits. This is your mid tone; your other choices of threads stem from here. Start stitching this area but consider the direction of the stitches. Consider the shape of your fruit. In this case the lemon is rounded, so you want the stitches to curve, which may require some smaller stitches overlapping to create the illusion of a smooth line. Using the mark-making skills you learnt earlier in the book, start stitching to the shape of the fruit.

Step 6

Once you have stitched using the first colour, take a look at your image – you're looking for the change in shade. Take the next shade down and start stitching. In order to blend your colours, you need to interrupt any harsh lines you have created. The stitches of one colour interspersed into the next colour should be very subtle and can take some

Add darker shades of yellow to block out where the shadows are on the lemons; small stitches will help blend the colours together.

practice. Continue to follow the directions of your stitches, with the intention that the viewer's eyes should follow the fruit in an uninterrupted way. The vision of the fruit should not be obstructed by stitches going in the wrong direction.

Take time to reflect. Stop stitching and assess your work. Are you happy? Do you need to adjust or add anything?

Step 7
The rest of the process is more of the same. Take the next shade darker or lighter and continue to blend, assessing your work at intervals.

Step 8
The white thread is for your lightest areas. This is often where the light is reflecting off a singular point on the skin of the fruit. This is really important to bring depth to your embroidery. The contrast between the highlighted areas and the darkest shade on your piece can make all the difference. Look carefully at where it is positioned on your image. You may be surprised at how little a space it is and how few stitches it will need, but it makes a difference all the same.

Step 9
Now you're nearly at completion, take your complementary colours, in this case some light blue shades and possibly some lilac tones. Like using white for highlighting, you will only require a small amount of thread and a few stitches. Add your complementary colours around the edges of the shadow areas. Don't add too much – the point of

Fill in more lighter mid tones to areas and start blending the shades using small stitches.

Start adding the lightest shades of yellow and white in the highlighted areas.

adding a complementary colour is to give your embroidery depth and encourage the contrast between dark and light. Knowing when to stop is something that can be a challenge, but with time you'll understand what is best for the image.

Practise and learn from your mistakes. Choose a different colour fruit and repeat the process; your complementary colours will be different, but a hands-on approach to embroidering the contrast between light and dark will be hugely beneficial, giving you every confidence you need to move forward and embroider larger still-life pieces. Some of my larger pieces have been the most challenging but also most rewarding embroideries. Complex compositions with an attention to light contrast are hugely rewarding when successfully translating the image into thread. Some of my largest embroideries have gained the most attention due to their exciting use of light and interesting composition, allowing me to use a wide range of colours and complementary shades to enhance an embroidery. Subject matter has an impact and we touch on that later in the book, but if it is executed badly it can be a disappointment.

Using blues and purples, stitch tiny amounts into the shadow of the lemon. Add the complementary colour, in this casea lilac, to the shadow of the lemons to help the image pop from the canvas.

CHAPTER 6

SPARK OF INSPIRATION: IGNITING YOUR MOOD AND MOTIVATION

In the vast landscape of creativity, inspiration serves as the guiding star, opening pathways to help you on your journey. However, the search for inspiration is not always straightforward; it often requires a deliberate and systematic approach to finding gems of creativity. In this chapter, we delve into the art of finding inspiration, the process of creating a mood board and its profound purpose in the realm of creative thinking and design.

EXPLORING THE HEIGHTS OF INSPIRATION

Inspiration, the elusive muse of creativity, can manifest itself in many forms and sources. It could be found in the budding of the cherry blossom in spring, the vibrant hues of a busy city street or the rhythmic beat of a neighbour's music. The key lies in fostering an acute awareness of one's surroundings and being receptive to the beauty and intricacies of everyday life. A lot of my inspiration over the years has come from my surroundings and the season of life I'm in. Being aware of the culture and life around you, whether it be a sombre mood or a whirlwind of chaos, is an important element of creativity.

The best way to cultivate a fertile ground for inspiration is to engage in activities that stimulate your senses and ignite your imagination. This may involve immersing yourself in nature, exploring art galleries, attending cultural events or simply observing the people and surroundings in your everyday life. By opening yourself to new experiences and perspectives, you can uncover a wealth of inspiration waiting to be discovered.

The Art of Creating a Mood Board

Gathering inspiration can sometimes be a little chaotic and at the start it is about bringing together lots of ideas and images ready to refine and discover what it is you're trying to portray. This is done in many ways, which will vary depending on your inspiration. Photos, magazine cuttings, exhibitions, experiences, sketches, swatches, colour palettes, written notes

– the list goes on. If there is a way of recording it as a visual, if there is a way of pinning it to a board as an instant visual, if it has inspired you in some way, keep it. This is where the creation of a mood board comes into play: an essential tool in the designer's arsenal for visual storytelling and conceptualisation.

A mood board is simply a collage of images, textures, colours and typography carefully curated to encapsulate the mood, tone and aesthetic vision of a design project. It serves as a visual roadmap, guiding you through the iterative process of ideation and refinement and is in my opinion a vital tool when designing and creating. There is no need for all your inspiration to be confined to your head or in pieces around your workspace; a mood board condenses and keeps you focused.

I used to collect old *Vogue* magazines. I did this for many years, the pages were rich with inspiration from photoshoots and the colours in adverts – I kept them all. It was a great tool for quickly finding visual stimuli, selecting those that resonate most strongly with the desired aesthetic and narrative. Creating a mood board is a fun way to collate all your inspiration in one place, arranging them all on a physical or digital canvas, forming a cohesive visual narrative that captures the essence of the design concept.

Unlocking the Purpose of Mood Boards

The purpose of a mood board extends far beyond its role as a mere collage of images; it is the cornerstone and catalyst of creativity, a compass for direction and a bridge between imagination and realisation. By consolidating disparate sources of inspiration into a unified visual language, mood boards provide you with a tangible reference point to guide your design decisions.

Moreover, mood boards foster collaboration and alignment within design teams, enabling people to see and share a vision and aesthetic direction. Whether presenting concepts to clients, pitching ideas to colleagues or soliciting feedback from peers, mood boards serve as powerful communication tools, facilitating dialogue and consensus-building.

Mood boards empower you to iterate rapidly and experiment with different visual elements, enabling you to explore alternative directions and refine your concepts. By providing a holistic overview of a design landscape, mood boards can encourage you to push the boundaries within your creativity and challenge conventional norms, potentially causing innovativeness in embroidery.

Finding inspiration can be sometimes the easiest thing and the hardest at the same time. You may find a subject or simply an object or a person that inspires your work. The process of exploring and refining can be both exhilarating and overwhelming.

Over time you may find a few avenues to help inspire your creativity, it will become clear that you gravitate towards a concept or area of particular interest. This may be when you start to define your signature style. The subject of your inspiration may reveal what makes your work unique.

Over the years, for me, inspiration has been the key to productive embroidery and has certainly defined who I am as an embroidery artist. Find something you are passionate about, interested in, overjoyed or fascinated by. If you are new to creating an original piece of embroidery, start small, with something you love to look at and with a version modest enough for you to stitch and accomplish in a short time. You want to inspire yourself to carry on and not be overwhelmed by the amount you have set yourself to do.

Sketching from life and sketching designs are an important part of the embroidery process if you're keen to embroider original pieces.

Peppers sketch.

A great way to start a collection is to create a mood board of the things that inspire you – if you start to see connections from one image to another and from phrases or words, keep editing and refining until you find a path you want to run down. Make a mood board the priority as you start gathering inspiration. Sketch books are an amazing way to keep track of what inspires you and are portable, ready for sketches, notes, photos and more. Designing and creating is a process and you rarely see a finished piece that hasn't had a period of development and refining.

Everyone's inspiration and form of gathering imagery will be different but set yourself the task of having all your inspiration for a collection or a project in one place. Here are some examples of how I have gathered and refined for each collection I have designed and embroidered.

Tropical bird mood board.

Nature mood board.

WHAT MAKES A COHESIVE COLLECTION?

We will go on to discuss collections in greater depth in Chapter 8, but here it is worth looking at the importance of a systematic approach to inspiration when formulating your ideas. When creating a collection, you want to display a wide range of examples of your exploration. Have you displayed and experimented to the extent that you are happy to share, does your message come across in each piece and as a collection? Have you yourself explored enough avenues with the techniques used? Are you happy with all the colours represented, do they all work well together and as stand-alone pieces? Each piece should be a representation of what you're trying to portray. A collection has to be critiqued as you go, always checking the relevance of each piece to the whole collection and its relevance on its own. If you were to take it out would it matter? Sometimes you may simply take a subject and showcase it in many ways, displaying the pieces in a similar way and it works brilliantly. Alternatively you may choose to have a main showstopping piece and some supporting smaller pieces that are equally stunning, but due to the scale of the smaller pieces they don't have the same impact. It may be that the smaller pieces are a close-up study of the bigger piece – the possibilities are endless, but the key is that they are clearly a part of the same body of work and by the same creator.

If you have been working systematically through this book and feel you are at the point of challenging yourself to create a collection, collating your inspirations and creating a mood board which pushes your comfort zone and challenges your skills, start formulating a collection and a plan of how this may come together. This chapter is designed to give you the encouragement to see that following a straightforward system of inspiration collation, refining and designing will leave you feeling ready to create an embroidery collection you're proud to showcase.

Tropical birds drawn with marker pens. Experimenting with colours can be a style point when collating a collection.

Floral inspired embroidery.

Miniature embroideries framed in recycled bottle caps.

KNOW WHEN YOU'RE FINISHED

Knowing when your piece is finished can be a conundrum. Sometimes the best thing to do is stop adding to it for a few days, put it away and don't look at it for a while. When you next take a look at the embroidery, instinct may tell you if it's finished or not. Often I will revisit a piece thinking it's finished, then with fresh eyes I can instinctively know what an embroidery is lacking – for me it's normally only a few hours more and then I'm happy to call it finished. This stage can be crucial. Sometimes we can be too close to our work to be critical or see what is needed to lift it to the next level. I often find that a simple colour contrast is what's needed to define an area of shadow or more texture to give depth. I actually put one of my biggest and most successful pieces Lost Love away for a few months. I became bored and lost sight of why I was creating it. One day I picked it up again and the journey of that piece then flew with a newfound respect for my initial inspiration, which pushed me through to the finish line.

Tomatoes on green gingham.

Ice creams in a row.

CHAPTER 7

MIX IT UP: EXPLORING MIXED MEDIA AND MACHINE EMBROIDERY

By now you have mastered the basics, you know how to get your ideas down and create a beautiful finished piece. Throughout the book we have looked closely at how to use threads and complete a design we are happy with and proud to display. As you experiment and challenge yourself, you should start to see your style develop and recognise key traits in your work.

This chapter explores beyond thread. By now you should be comfortable with threads if you've completed some of the projects in previous chapters. It's important even when you have mastered a craft that you continue to grow. This chapter should encourage you to keep exploring and stay excited about what your next project is, pushing yourself out of your comfort zone so your work can excel.

As an embroidery enthusiast, I have often found myself captivated by the intricate art of stitching. However, the world of textile arts is vast, offering a plethora of techniques that beautifully complement embroidery. In this chapter, we embark on a journey to explore other mediums such as beading, appliqué and paint, discovering their unique charm and potential for creative expression alongside your new-found love of embroidery.

Combining embroidery with other mediums opens avenues for artistic experimentation and innovation. Mixed media embroidery allows stitchers to break free from traditional constraints, blending different textures, colours and techniques to create dynamic and captivating pieces of art. By venturing beyond traditional embroidery techniques and embracing the richness of other mediums, we open doors to endless possibilities for creative exploration and self-expression. So, let your imagination soar and dive into the world of mixed media stitchery!

INTRODUCING PAINT

Using paint on fabric before embroidering can significantly enhance the depth and visual interest of your piece. There are different types of paint that can be used effectively. Painting fabric before embroidering serves several purposes; it can add depth and dimension when used for the background of a piece, making the embroidery stand out more. A painted layer can complement and enhance the embroidery design adding complexity and richness. Paint can also provide a contrasting backdrop.

Watercolour paint is an excellent choice for cotton canvas fabric; its fluidity allows for a range of effects, from soft washes to more intense colour. Watercolour paint remains relatively thin, making it easy to sew through, allowing your needle to glide smoothly. Painting a canvas before you start applying embroidery doesn't have to follow your design precisely. Instead, it can serve as an abstract or contrasting layer that enhances the overall piece.

Acrylic paint, on the other hand, offers a bold and vibrant enhancement to your fabric pieces but requires some considerations. Acrylic is thicker than watercolour, which can make stitching through it more challenging. It is best to mix acrylic paint with a fabric medium which will make it more flexible and supple, reducing the risk of the fabric becoming too stiff and cracking. Adding a textile medium to the acrylic will make it easier for the needle to pass through a painted area. Using acrylic on the back of a jacket, combined with embroidery, can create striking effects. The boldness of the paint can minimise the amount of stitching needed, as the painted design itself can be prominent.

Embroidering on Painted Fabric

- Always pre-wash your fabric to remove any sizing or chemicals that might interfere with paint adherence.
- Experiment on a small fabric swatch to see how the paint behaves and how easy it is to stitch through once dry.
- Once the paint is dry, consider heat setting it (following the paint manufacturer's instructions) to ensure it remains permanent and washable.
- Always use a sharp needle that can easily penetrate the painted fabric without causing damage.
- Remember that the painted layer doesn't have to be perfect or match your embroidery exactly. The beauty lies in the combination of textures and colours.
- Acrylics can be a great way of painting the background of an embroidered canvas before you start to embroider; it's an effective way of filling a large space and it creates a great contrast in your work.

Adding paint to fabric provides you with a great base to start embroidering on.

M&M packet with acrylic painted canvas. Painting a background can give a focus to the embroidery and the contrast helps lift the embroidery off the canvas.

A FEW IDEAS AND CONSIDERATIONS

Layering using paint

- Use watercolour for the initial layer to create a soft, textured background, then add acrylic accents for bold details.
- Combine paint, embroidery and other embellishments such as beads or sequins for a mixed-media masterpiece.
- For themed pieces, let the paint set the scene, such as a watercolour sky for an embroidered landscape or a bold acrylic design for a modern art piece.
- By incorporating painting techniques with your embroidery, you can create unique, visually stunning pieces that stand out. The combination of paint and thread brings together the best of both worlds, allowing for endless creativity and expression.

Branching Out

Pairing watercolour with embroidery can create stunning and unique pieces of art, blending the delicate transparency of watercolour with the tactile richness of embroidery. Here's a guide on how to effectively combine these two techniques to enhance your artwork.

Choose Your Materials Wisely

- Use watercolour paints that have vibrant pigments and are lightfast to ensure the longevity of your artwork. Opt for embroidery floss or threads in colours that complement your watercolour palette.
- Plan your piece; sketch your design lightly on the fabric using a pencil. This will serve as a guideline for both your painting and embroidery.
- Consider how the two mediums will interact and overlap. Leave areas for embroidery that will enhance and complement the watercolour elements.
- Start with watercolour; begin by painting your watercolour base layer. Apply washes of colour using a light touch, building up layers gradually to achieve depth and dimension.
- Allow each layer to dry completely before adding the next to prevent colours from bleeding into each other, unless this is a design choice. Experiment with techniques such as wet-on-wet and wet-on-dry to create different textures and effects in your watercolour painting.
- Incorporate embroidery; once your watercolour painting is dry, begin adding embroidery stitches to enhance and embellish the design. Choose stitches that will complement the shapes and lines of your watercolour elements. For example, use satin stitch for smooth areas and French knots for texture.
- Consider using embroidery to add details such as outlines, highlights or additional layers of colour that may be difficult to achieve with watercolour alone.

Combine Techniques

Experiment with combining watercolour and embroidery techniques to create unique effects. For example, you can use watercolour washes as a background for embroidered motifs or incorporate embroidered patterns into your watercolour painting.

Be mindful of the balance between the two mediums, ensuring that neither overwhelms the other and that they work together harmoniously to enhance the overall composition.

Practice and Experiment

Like any art form, combining watercolour and embroidery requires practice and experimentation to develop your own unique style and techniques. Don't be afraid to make mistakes or try new approaches. Some of the most interesting and innovative artwork comes from pushing the boundaries and exploring the possibilities of different mediums.

By following these steps and allowing your creativity to flourish, you can create beautiful and expressive artworks that seamlessly blend the delicate transparency of watercolour with the tactile richness of embroidery. Experimentation, practice and a willingness to explore new techniques will ultimately lead to stunning and unique results.

Close-up of Wild Flowers embroidery. Hand-stretched unprimed canvas with acrylic and cotton thread.

Painted and embroidered Bold Flower.

Wild Daisy paint and thread embroidered canvas.

DIVING INTO BEADING: ADDING SPARKLE TO STITCHERY

Beadwork has been intertwined with human history for millennia, adorning garments, accessories and ceremonial objects with its dazzling allure. Incorporating beads into embroidery elevates the texture and dimension of a piece, adding a touch of opulence and intricacy.

Beads come in various shapes, sizes and materials, from delicate seed beads to lustrous pearls and shimmering sequins. It may suit your style to choose chunky wooden beads – the choices will become a design decision.

There are a number of techniques you can use when adding beads to your embroidered work, including couching, where beads are secured onto the fabric with stitches, and bead embroidery, where beads are stitched directly onto the fabric surface, creating intricate patterns and textures.

It's worth experimenting and trying out a range of beads, they can give your work extra depth and texture depending on their size, form and material.

Embroidered and beaded close-up.

Embroidered trucker caps.

Mini mixed media pin broaches. Combining beads with embroidery makes for beautifully textured embroideries and one-of-a-kind pieces.

APPLIQUÉ: A PATCHWORK OF CREATIVITY

In the vast tapestry of textile artistry, one technique stands out for its versatility, elegance and potential for artistic expression: appliqué. Rooted in centuries of tradition yet adaptable to contemporary design, appliqué offers a canvas for imagination to flourish. When combined with the intricate charm of embroidery, it unveils a realm where stitches weave stories, colours dance and textures speak volumes.

At its essence, appliqué involves the layering of fabric onto a base material to create decorative motifs or patterns. This technique transcends the boundaries of functionality, evolving into a medium for storytelling, cultural expression and personal style. From quilts to garments, accessories to home décor, appliqué embellishes our world with a touch of artistry.

Embroidering patches that can be applied to clothing and soft furnishings is useful if a fabric does not lend itself to a lot of stitching. Patches are also removable.

Appliqué, derived from the French word *appliquer*, meaning 'to apply', involves attaching fabric pieces onto a base fabric to create decorative motifs or patterns. This versatile technique will open doors to endless possibilities of creativity and craftsmanship, allowing you to experiment with fabric combinations, shapes and textures. Appliqué can transform textile projects with beauty, character and a handmade touch. Appliqué can also be a practical technique for repairing and upcycling old or damaged textiles. By covering holes or stains with creative patches, you can give new life to well-loved items.

Fabrics for appliqué can vary from cotton and silk to wool and felt, offering a diverse palette to play with. Fusible webbing or hand stitching is used to affix the appliqué pieces onto the base fabric.

Techniques

Machine appliqué is when a sewing machine is used to stitch around the edges of the appliqué shapes, securing them to the base fabric. Hand appliqué, on the other hand, involves meticulous hand stitching, often employing techniques like needle-turn or blanket stitch for a polished finish.

When paired with embroidery, appliqué forms a harmonious symphony of stitches and fabrics. Embroidery stitches serve not only to secure the appliqué pieces but also to enhance their visual appeal. Whether it's a delicate satin stitch outlining a floral motif or the intricate detail of a French knot accentuating a textured fabric, embroidery elevates the art of appliqué to new heights.

Choosing Fabrics and Designs

Selecting the right fabrics is crucial for successful appliqué-embroidery projects. Consider the weight, texture and colour compatibility of fabrics to ensure cohesion in your design. Experiment with combinations of cotton, silk, wool and felt to achieve the desired effects. Remember, the interplay of fabrics enriches the visual and tactile experience of your artwork.

Tools of the Trade

Equipping yourself with the right tools simplifies the process and enhances the outcome of your appliqué-embroidery endeavours. Invest in quality scissors for precise cutting, embroidery hoops for tension control and needles suitable for various fabrics and stitch types. A reliable sewing machine equipped with appliqué-friendly features can expedite your projects without compromising on craftsmanship.

Techniques and Tips

Mastering appliqué-embroidery techniques requires patience, practice and a willingness to explore. Start by sketching your design on paper, then transfer it onto the base fabric using preferred methods such as tracing or printing. Experiment with different appliqué methods, including raw-edge, turned-edge and reverse appliqué to achieve diverse effects.

Bringing Your Vision to Life

As you explore the endless possibilities of appliqué-embroidery, allow your creativity to guide you. Embrace imperfections as opportunities for innovation, and let your intuition be your compass. Whether you're embellishing a quilt, adorning a garment or crafting a work of art, infuse each stitch with intention and passion. Remember, the journey of creation is as enriching as the destination.

In the intricate dance of appliqué and embroidery, every stitch will form a cohesive, attractive composition. Through experimentation, dedication and a touch of imagination, you will start to push boundaries. Gather your fabrics to form a mini library of colours and texture, play around with pairing threads that blend and contrast with your selections. The appliqué stage should come before you start adding embroidery and some planning is required early on in your designing of the embroidery. A level of precision and accuracy is required when appliqué is used to ensure stunning results. Ensuring your appliqués are absolutely flat and pinned or glued to the base fabric securely will make a difference in the finish of your embroidered appliqué piece.

Exploring Other Mediums

- Start small: Experiment with beads or appliqué on small-scale projects like patches or embellishments before tackling larger pieces.
- Embrace creativity: Don't be afraid to mix and match different mediums to achieve unique effects and textures.
- Practise patience: Beading and appliqué require precision and attention to detail, so take your time and enjoy the process.
- Learn from others: Join embroidery groups or workshops to learn new techniques and gain inspiration from fellow stitchers.

The possibilities are endless. Edit, refine and edit again. Consider your decision making with care and attention to detail, get a second opinion. As creatives, we quite often get too close to our work and lose sight of where we are going. Taking a step back and getting a critical opinion are so valuable.

FREEHAND MACHINE EMBROIDERY

Freehand machine embroidery, also known as free-motion embroidery, is a dynamic and creative method of embroidery that allows artists and crafters to bring their intricate designs to life using a sewing machine. This technique offers the freedom to create detailed and personalised designs, making it an appealing craft for both beginners and experienced embroiderers. Give yourself the chance to explore the benefits of freehand machine embroidery and dive into the process. To help you experiment with guidance, there are two projects involving the use of machine embroidery; the first is embroidered napkins and the second a cushion cover. These projects will also cover how to incorporate appliqué into your work with the chance to add beaded details. So, what are the benefits of freehand machine embroidery?

Creative Freedom

Freehand machine embroidery allows you to draw with your sewing machine, giving you the freedom to create any design imaginable. Unlike traditional embroidery, which relies on preset stitches and patterns, freehand machine embroidery lets you control the movement of the fabric and the direction of the stitches, enabling a more personalised and unique creation. There are industrial machines that are built specifically for this free motion, they are a joy to use and give you freedom to explore. On a domestic machine you are a little bit limited, but it will give you enough freedom to broaden your creativity.

Versatility

This technique can be applied to a wide range of projects and fabrics. Whether you want to embellish clothing, home decor items or accessories, freehand machine embroidery is adaptable to various textures and surfaces. You can also use dissolvable fabric which will leave you with only your embroidery stitches.

Speed

Once you become proficient, freehand machine embroidery can be much faster than hand embroidery. The sewing machine's speed combined with your dexterity allows for quicker completion of intricate designs. It has a very different texture to hand embroidery and like all design choices, there are decisions to be made and tested before knowing if it's the right technique for a project.

Accessibility

You don't need specialised embroidery machines to start; a regular sewing machine with the ability to drop the feed dogs (the teeth that move the fabric) is sufficient. This makes it accessible to anyone with a standard sewing machine. If you do have the opportunity to try out any embroidery machines like an Irish or a Cornelli, jump at the opportunity, it's a challenge well worth trying.

Personalisation

This technique enables you to add a personal touch to gifts, clothing and home decor items, making them unique. It may be that you choose to combine this technique with hand embroidery or with appliqué. You may even consider embellishing your freehand embroidery too.

Getting Started with Freehand Machine Embroidery

You will need:

- Sewing machine: A machine that allows you to drop or cover the feed dogs is essential. Most modern sewing machines have this feature.
- Embroidery hoop: While optional, an embroidery hoop can help stabilise the fabric and maintain tension. Test your fabric – you will have more freedom if it is not retained in a hoop but you need the fabric to stay firm and not pucker or pull when stitching.
- Embroidery foot (darning foot): This special foot allows for better visibility and movement of the fabric. In the past, I have gone footless which is great, but you need to be cautious and vigilant as the needle is very exposed.
- Fabric: Choose a fabric that is suitable for your project. Cotton, linen and denim are great choices for beginners. But as mentioned before you can use this technique

Consider using simple patterned fabric for appliqué. Appliqué is a great way to block an area before stitching.

on most fabrics – test first. Some fabrics may require a slower pace when stitching than others, to limit snagging.

- Stabiliser: A stabiliser is used to keep the fabric from puckering and shifting. Tear-away, cut-away or water-soluble stabilisers can be used depending on the fabric and project.
- Thread: Embroidery thread or any high-quality sewing thread will work. Rayon and polyester threads are popular for their sheen and durability. This will be down to your preference and design choice; metallic and silk threads are great but may require some patience and tension adjustments.
- Marking tools: Fabric markers, chalk or pencils to draw your designs on the fabric. You can also use the transfer techniques to get your image onto the fabric.

Setting Up Your Sewing Machine

- Install the embroidery foot (also known as the quilter's foot). Attach the embroidery foot to your machine. This foot has a spring and an open toe for better control and visibility.
- Lower the feed dogs.
- Check your machine's manual to learn how to lower or cover the feed dogs. This step is crucial as it allows you to move the fabric freely in any direction.
- Adjust tension and stitch length.
- Set your machine to a straight stitch with a medium stitch length. You may need to adjust the tension based on your fabric and thread.

Practice

Before starting your main project, practise on a scrap piece of your chosen fabric to get comfortable with controlling the fabric and creating consistent stitches. Draw simple shapes or lines to trace with your machine, focusing on maintaining even stitch lengths and smooth movements.

Applying a patch and embellishing a cushion cover can transform your home furnishings. Here's a step-by-step guide to help you through the process, including making and embroidering the patch and appliquéing it onto the cushion.

Coloured fabric. Having scraps and larger pieces of different colours is a good idea when experimenting with appliqué.

Mixed box of machine threads. Having a wide variety of colours for machine embroidery will give you the chance to explore ideas freely.

MACHINE-EMBROIDERED APPLIQUÉ

You will need:
(For the patch)
Fabric for the patch
Embroidery floss
Embroidery hoop
Embroidery needle
Scissors
Fabric marker or pencil
Stabiliser (optional)
(For the cushion cover)
Plain cushion cover
Thread matching the patch fabric
Sewing machine or needle
Pins or fabric glue

Step 1
Draw or print out the design you want to embroider for your patch. Consider the scale in relation to the cushion; a larger patch will have a good impact but it may be that your design requires a small, discrete patch. Transfer the design onto the fabric using a fabric marker or pencil.

Prepare the fabric and cut a piece slightly larger than the design. Place in an embroidery hoop to keep it taut.

Machine embroidery cushion project.

Transfer image to fabric ready for stitching.

Embroider the design. Choose a stitch or a few stitches but consider the function of a cushion; you need to ensure the threads are at a low risk of being pulled or caught.

Step 2
Start by adding a stabiliser to the back of your design area. Using the freehand embroidery technique, start embroidering and filling in the colour on your patch. This will vary depending on your design.

Step 3
Start by stitching all the same colour if this is possible with your design – you want to change the colour thread on your machine as little as you can as it can be a timely process. Make sure as you finish each colour, you back stitch over your embroidery to secure ends.

Step 4
Once the embroidery is complete, cut out the patch, leaving a small border around the design. At this point you need to apply the patch to the front of your cushion cover. You can do this with freehand machine embroidery, alternatively you can put the feet back up on your machine, choose a zig-zag stitch and sew the patch on this way. Place the patch in place and pin into position, ensuring it lays flat with minimal movement. You can also use a fabric glue to help hold it in place if you prefer. Once the patch is stitched into place, it's

Begin to stitch, following the transfer marks.

Sew the image using freehand machine embroidery.

Sew on to the cushion.

Ta da! The completed cushion.

time to make up the rest of the cushion. Sew the zip in place at one end of your square cushion, ensure the right sides of the fabric are together through this sewing-up process. Once the challenge of sewing a zip in is complete, sew up the rest of the cushion cover along the seam allowance, trim the corners and turn through, carefully pushing the corners out. Your custom-decorated cushion cover is now ready to enhance your home décor!

Make an Appliqué Cushion Cover

- Choose fabric and floss colours that complement the cushion cover.
- Practise your embroidery on a scrap piece of fabric if you're new to it.
- Ensure all embellishments are securely attached to withstand use.
- You could choose, at the making-up stage, to sew in trim to the seams as you construct your cushion.
- Enjoy your beautifully personalised cushion cover!

EMBROIDERED NAPKINS

You will need:

Plain cotton or linen napkins
Embroidery thread in various colours
Fabric marker
Stabiliser
Embroidery hoop (optional)

Step 1

Wash and iron the napkins so they are ready for sewing, washing your fabric for the first time. Before you do any embroidery on the napkin, it is important to wash them as the fabric will always shrink a little. Ironing your napkins will give you a great start, ensuring a smooth surface. Embroidered napkins are a beautiful addition to any special meal.

Step 2

Think of small embroideries you would like to have on a napkin – they may be food or flora based, or perhaps a quirky monogram could be fun for a personal gift. Draw up your design to scale, ready to transfer to the fabric.

Step 3

Before you stitch anything, consider carefully your colour placement. You'll need a plan to reduce the thread changing as much as possible and to keep the monogram neat. Have this plan ready for your sewing stage.

Embroidered cocktail napkin.

Create simple designs.

Transfer your designs to the fabric, and collect together your chosen colour threads.

Hoop up and start stitching.

Step 4
Place the stabiliser on the back of the embroidery area. Keep this as minimal as possible, but ensure it covers the whole area. Draw or transfer your design – remember if your way of marking the fabric is permanent, you will need to be sure to cover the area with stitches.

Step 5
Use a fabric marker to draw your design on the napkin. Simple floral motifs, monograms or geometric patterns work well for beginners. Next, set up the machine. Place the napkin into the hoop, with the area you want to embroider at the centre. The hoop will keep the fabric taut and help you to keep control of your stitching. Attach the embroidery foot and lower the feed dogs. Place the napkin with the stabiliser under the foot. If you don't have a quilter's/embroidery foot, sewing without a foot will do the job but isn't quite as good.

Step 6
Begin at one end of your design, gently moving the fabric as you sew. Keep your movements slow and steady to maintain consistent stitches. Unlike stitching by hand, where you can do a few stitches and change your threads frequently, machine embroidery needs a plan. It's advised that you draw

up a design with a helpful key to what colours are placed in each area. As you start out with your machine freehand embroidery, try to block out the colours on your design to keep it looking neat and to reduce the changes of threads. As you stitch, follow your plan. Follow the lines of your design, changing thread colours as needed to add details and dimension.

Step 7
Once the design is complete, trim any loose threads. At this point I would dab a tiny bit of textile glue across the back of the embroidered area, as the napkin may be a high-use object and this will help prevent wear to the embroidery. Press the napkins ready to use. A set of beautifully embroidered personalised napkins makes for a very special gift with endless design possibilities.

Freehand machine embroidery is a versatile and rewarding craft that allows for immense creative freedom. With the right tools, practice and patience, you can create stunning and unique pieces that showcase your artistic flair. Embrace the learning process, experiment with different techniques, and most importantly, have fun bringing your designs to life.

Planning a machine embroidery can be a key part of your process. Like any creative endeavour it's important to make the process your own and experiment to uncover your full potential with this technique. If drawing is a strong element of your creativity, consider embroidering without a plan, and drawing with your machine as if it were a pencil. Use your fabric like a sketch book and explore the possibilities.

Creating a background with varying fabrics before you stitch can give an embroidery depth. You could upcycle clothes and recycle fabrics to create sustainable embroidered pieces. The possibilities are endless; go and explore and enjoy them.

An embroidery foot will help achieve a good result.

Press and the cocktail napkins are ready to use.

CHAPTER 8

CURATED CREATIONS: TURNING COLLECTIONS INTO ART

Embroidery is an art form that encourages creativity to flourish and creating an embroidery collection is a challenging but fulfilling endeavour. This chapter will bring to life all the knowledge and skills you have gained throughout the book and provide you with a step-by-step guide on forming a collection from concept to presentation. Research is essential so you can become immersed in your concept and ideas. Be intentional with how you engage and expose yourself to culture and experiences. You can feel overwhelmed when you find an area of inspiration; the key is to be clear and concise in what your narrative is before you start finalising ideas for your collection.

Embroidery is an art form and transcends mere stitching to become a medium of expression, imbued with emotions, stories and creativity. We find this through the rich history of embroidery across the globe. Crafting a coherent embroidery collection requires a fusion of inspiration, research and technique. Mood boards serve as indispensable tools for this journey, guiding you from initial ideation to the creation of a harmonious collection. The innovative use of thread as paint adds a dynamic dimension to embroidery, elevating it beyond conventional boundaries. This chapter explores the significance of mood boards in the creative process and offers insights into refining research to develop a cohesive embroidery collection and how to present your work in a professional and cohesive way.

Delve deeper into the historical, cultural or thematic significance of the elements you have chosen. Research traditional embroidery techniques, symbolism and motifs associated with the chosen theme. Drawing inspiration from diverse sources enriches the narrative of the collection and adds depth to your artistic expression. You can do this in a variety of ways – it will of course depend on what your subject matter is, the key is to immerse yourself in all the information you can find so when it comes to refining, you have a large body of work to use. Sketches, photos, exhibitions, swatches, magazine cuttings and found objects are all going to give you a rich ground on which to base your collection. Once you've collected and researched, which may take a few weeks, you should start to see some ideas stand out. Refining takes time and practice; your aim is to pick out key elements for further development. From this point start creating samples and sketches in order to design your embroideries. When making a collection, not every piece needs to tell the whole story but it should sit very comfortably next to another piece within the collection. Remember, as discussed in Chapter 6, mood boards serve as invaluable tools in the creative process, guiding you from inspiration to execution with clarity and coherence. By refining research and embracing innovative techniques, embroidery collections can transcend conventional boundaries, offering a fresh perspective on this timeless art form.

Experimenting and Creating Samples

Innovative artists are constantly pushing the boundaries of traditional embroidery techniques, incorporating unconventional materials to redefine the medium. One such technique gaining traction is the use of thread as paint. This is a style I have developed over years of practice; I like to see the box of threads like a palette of paint and often imagine my needle almost like a paint brush, my stitches changing direction and creating texture as I work.

Try out a variety of techniques with a variety of stitches. Before you make decisions it's important to push boundaries in preparation for concluding what your collection or embroidered pieces will be. All the points of the process are important, but sampling is about trying and testing techniques so you can achieve the best result but also you gain experience and know how fabrics, scale, threads and techniques interact with each other.

Start Developing a Coherent Embroidery Collection

Samples are not fully finished pieces and it may be you have a tiny sample with a new stitch you have found, but the importance of testing is the key to a well-curated collection. Experiment with combining traditional embroidery stitches with your own style of stitch. Create samples incorporating other mediums with embroidery. You could combine paint embellishments to create visually captivating textures and patterns, or test out a variety of fabrics and adornments, considering how each piece contributes to the overarching theme or story.

Armed with refined research and experimental techniques, it's time to translate concepts into tangible creations. Start by sketching preliminary designs, exploring composition, scale and placement of embroidery motifs. Referencing the mood board for guidance, refine the designs to ensure consistency and coherence within the collection. Aim for a balance between unity and diversity, allowing individual pieces to stand out while contributing to the collective harmony of the collection.

With careful curation and experimentation, you can craft collections that resonate with depth, emotion and creativity, enriching the tapestry of embroidered storytelling.

Selecting Designs to Form a Collection

It's important to be excited and passionate about your ideas as this will be your motivation to complete each part of your collection. If you lose interest in your ideas, they will become very difficult to complete. As you have sketched up ideas and taken photos, try out a variety of compositions. Maybe you have a great photo with excellent attention to light and you're excited to stitch your image, consider your canvas and where the image will sit; how much space is around it? Don't just place your image in the centre, try a variety of positions.

The realities for stitching or combining some mediums may prove not to have an impact or just be wrong for your collection. It's important to test so you can see if it has potential or whether it's not going to work. As you start to collate your collection, see if all your images sit well together – again, this process can take a while. I sometimes find I have a few ideas that I know I want to run with, but my collection is not fully formed. This is fine. It is important that you can be self-critical; edit and assess your work as you go. Be sure of your idea and direction but be flexible with the outcomes.

Below is a check list for creating your own coherent, well-curated collection:

- Collect your visuals, swatches, colours, magazine cuttings, photos, textures and so on.

- Create your mood board including a wide variety of visuals and textures. Include notes of any ideas you have – you don't need to use them all. More is better at this point.
- Pull out the essentials that simplify but define your concept, refine so your concept is clear but not so much that you lose impact. A good guide is that you should not need to explain too much.
- Create sketch ideas of what you want to embroider, leave notes of what to use at different points. Don't rely on your memory.
- Select some designs with test samples to accompany the ideas.
- Draw up and photograph your designs and ideas ready for transfer. Do a load with tiny variations and pick the most effective images.
- Choose your fabrics (this may have been part of your design process already) and how you're going to present your design – this will determine whether you need to stretch your own canvas. Assess how much fabric you will need for a piece.
- The fun bit; start stitching and bring your pieces to life.

When you can call a piece finished, it's time to frame and present. Keep reading for some helpful tips on how to present your embroideries.

Drawers of rainbow colour threads. Extending your collections of threads will give you the opportunity to experiment and push boundaries.

Study of an eye, experimenting with colour.

Embroidered eye, mixed-media watercolour and thread.

Finished embroidered eye. Experimenting will help you feel comfortable with pairing colours and help understand colour theory more clearly.

Flower meadow embroidery with hand-painted yellow hoop. Once the back is fitted with felt, you can sew or glue a picture hoop on the back ready to hang; alternatively, you can string up a ribbon or cord for hanging.

PRESENTATION

So you have been through all the processes of how to design and stitch your piece and it's finished, but now what? The answer is not to tuck it away and forget you spent hours lovingly stitching something beautiful. Framing and presenting your work can be one of the most daunting parts of the process, but equally one of the most important and rewarding.

Framing and presenting your embroidery is a crucial part of finishing and preparing your work for an audience. If this aspect is well considered and executed to a high standard, your embroidery will be received with much more respect than if it is thrown together without care or thought. This process will vary for each piece and may take a while, which is why it can often be put off and avoided. However, if you rush this part of your process, it will be noticeable. You want your audience to be wowed at the first sight of your work. Your embroidery should always be the focus, and distractions caused by an ill-fitting frame, hoop or poorly measured finish will only detract from your stunning work.

Lost Love detail. This piece is a wall hanging and fitted with a sturdy dowl through the loop at the top, ready to be hung as a large tapestry.

Influential Women, cotton thread on cotton.

So where to begin? As we have discovered throughout this book, with every step of the way there are critical questions to ask yourself. Each piece of work is different from the next, so it's not a one-size-fits-all approach. You may be working on a series of pieces that you purposely want to present in the same frame or manner, which is absolutely fine and a great design consideration. In this case, your design process will be reversed a little and as you choose your designs, you'll consider your options much earlier in the process. You may have a rough idea of how you'll frame or mount your work, and again, this may influence your choice of fabric, the size of the embroidery and potentially the yarn you will use.

I find that I try to put this part off as long as possible because it's not very creative and I feel the pressure of perfection. I'm not built that way, but I know how important it is to be precise, accurate and have immaculate attention to detail at this point. Occasionally, I have an idea of how it will be presented and then change my mind as I end a project. This, of course, is not ideal in some circumstances, as sometimes you may be limited by the excess fabric available. It's always a bit of a new learning curve, but as I have said many times throughout this process, it's essential to know your own mind, understand how you like to work, and what keeps you excited and enjoying embroidery. Never try to shoehorn a process in a way someone else has done it if you find it a struggle. Take the basics and turn them into your own process. My suggestions are simply ideas for you to make your own.

Whether you're displaying a delicate watercolour painting or an intricately embroidered piece, selecting the ideal frame can make all the difference. Explore the various types of framing options available and try different styles so you can select the best one for your artworks.

Understanding Different Types of Frames

Before diving into specifics, it's essential to understand the different types of frames available:

- Wooden frames: These are classic and versatile, offering a wide range of finishes and styles, from sleek and modern to ornate and traditional.
- Metal frames: Typically used for contemporary artworks, metal frames provide a minimalist and sleek look. They come in various finishes like matte, brushed or polished.
- Acrylic frames: These frames offer a modern and minimalist appearance. They are lightweight and often used for artworks where you want the frame to be less noticeable.
- Shadow box frames: Ideal for three-dimensional artworks like sculptures or heavily textured pieces, shadow box frames provide depth and space around the artwork.
- Floater frames: These are designed to make the artwork appear as if it's floating within the frame, creating a contemporary and elegant presentation.

Choosing the Right Frame for Embroidered Artworks

Embroidered artworks require careful consideration when it comes to framing due to their unique characteristics. Here are some framing options that work best for embroidered pieces:

- Matting: Matting is crucial for embroidered artworks as it helps to keep the fabric away from the glass, preventing any potential damage. Opt for acid-free mat boards to ensure the longevity of your artwork.
- Wooden frames: Wooden frames with intricate details or a rustic finish can beautifully complement the craftsmanship of embroidered artworks, adding warmth and character to the piece.
- Shadow box frames: Since embroidered artworks often have a three-dimensional quality, shadow box frames provide the perfect depth to showcase the intricacies of the stitching. They also offer protection without flattening the fabric.
- Floating frames: For a modern and minimalist look, floating frames can be an excellent choice for embroidered artworks. The space around the artwork allows the intricate details to shine without any distraction.
- Custom frames: Consider getting a custom frame made specifically for your embroidered artwork. This way, you can tailor the frame's design, size and materials to perfectly complement the style and dimensions of your piece.

Banana; cotton thread embroidered on primed canvas and stretched over bars. Framed in a floating frame.

Box-framed English tea-inspired embroideries.

When selecting a frame for your embroidered artwork, it's essential to consider the overall aesthetic you wish to achieve. Pay attention to the colours, textures and style of the frame, ensuring that it enhances rather than overwhelms the artwork. Additionally, always use archival-quality materials to protect your piece from damage caused by light, humidity or other environmental factors.

By carefully selecting the right frame, you can elevate the presentation of your embroidered artwork, turning it into a timeless masterpiece that will be cherished for years to come.

With all the considerations and options you have before you, you're sure to find a style of framing that best suits your way of working. Experimenting is important but also talking to professional framers and other artists is a great way to broaden your knowledge and understand what framing can do to elevate your work.

I have included practical step-by-step guides on how to finish your embroideries. They include finishing and backing your hooped embroidery, backing an embroidery ready for framing and stretching your own fabric of choice onto stretcher bars.

Embroidery on a canvas with hanging fittings attached. Attaching fittings straight on to the canvas can enable your embroidery to be hung with limited effort.

Mangoes on flowers.

Using the Hoop to Frame

Framing your embroidery using the hoop itself is probably the simplest way to present your work. It requires only a few additional tools and materials. You effectively use your hoop as a frame, which can either be strung up with ribbon or hooked onto a wall.

Once you're satisfied that your embroidery is complete, you will need to gather the excess fabric to the back neatly, preparing to sew on a back panel. Felt is the simplest material

Hand-painted embroidery hoops are a great way to present your embroideries, with the wide range of sizes of hoop available and the variation of colours.

A felt back panel is a neat way to finish your work.

Gather the excess fabric on the back of your embroidery using a running stitch. This is then gently pulled to gather the fabric neatly towards the centre of the back ready for the felt back.

to use for finishing the back of your hoop. This process may take longer than you expect, but it's worth taking the time to achieve presentable results.

Step 1
Take a long length of thread, enough to go around your hoop twice. It's important that the thread is in one piece to avoid having to tie it off and start a new thread.

Step 2
Cut the excess fabric around your hoop to a depth of about 4cm–6cm. If you leave much more than this, it will still work but may prove tricky to achieve a clean finish.

Step 3
Tie a knot at the end of your thread, making sure it's big enough to not pull through the fabric. Pull your needle through the fabric on the back of your design, approximately halfway between the hoop and the cut edge of your fabric. Using a running stitch with about 1cm stitch length, sew around the circle but do not finish or tie off the thread. Instead, leave it long.

Gently pull the thread to gather the fabric around the back of the hoop. Pull the thread tight until the fabric cannot be gathered any further, then tie the thread securely to the fabric. If you were to remove the outer hoop at this point, the fabric would keep its shape but lose a little tension.

Step 4

Cut a piece of felt about 0.5cm smaller than your inner hoop. Draw around the hoop and then, when you cut it out, trim an extra 0.5cm from your drawn circle.

Ensure your outer hoop is tight and attached to your inner hoop. Place the felt on the back where you have gathered the excess fabric. You can now see how the back of your embroidery will look.

Step 5

Take a matching thread, or a contrasting one if you want to make a statement on the back. Tie a knot at the end of a long piece of thread.

Using a slip stitch, sew the felt to the edge of your embroidery fabric just inside the outer hoop. Each stitch should be about 0.5cm apart and each stitch length around 0.25cm.

Stitch the slip stitch in a full circle around the back of your embroidery hoop, then tie it off. Thread your needle back through and out of the felt backing, trapping the loose thread behind the felt cover.

Now your hoop is finished and ready to hang with a neatly covered back.

Presentable back of a finished embroidery. Slip-stitched felt on the back of bamboo hoop.

Framing an Unhooped Piece

Whether you are considering framing using an off-the-shelf frame or a bespoke one, I recommend this technique for finishing your embroidery and preparing it for framing.

If you are using this technique, there are things to think about before starting your design and stitching. Choose a fabric with a sturdy structure and preferably no stretch. This method allows you to work on a large piece and move your hoop around the fabric to the areas you are embroidering. It's important that during the embroidery stage, you put your fabric under tension as you stitch without pulling it out of shape. As you move your hoop, check that your fabric lays as flat as possible after each move. Puckering or ripples may occur if you have not stretched your fabric in the hoop well enough, which could potentially cause problems when you stretch your embroidery for framing.

Step 1

Regardless of whether you are using a shop-bought or bespoke frame for your finished piece, you need to stretch it over some thin hardboard. Hardboard works well for me but you can use a different board if you prefer. Cut your board to the finished size you want using a craft knife, set square and ruler to ensure straight lines and right angles. This board should sit snugly just inside your frame.

Step 2

Depending on your embroidery fabric, you may want to make a cotton sleeve for your board. This step is optional but can prevent the colour of the board from showing through and compromising the look of your finished embroidery. Cut the fabric of your embroidered piece 10cm–15cm larger all the way around to allow for stretching. Using pinking shears can prevent the fabric from fraying as much as it would with a regular straight cut.

Step 3

Place your fabric face down on a clear flat surface and position the board on top, ensuring you are happy with the placement of your embroidery. Using a long, sturdy thread (such as a six-strand cotton embroidery thread or pearl cotton), start stitching with a lacing technique from top to bottom.

Aim to insert your needle approximately halfway between the cut edge and the board's edge. As you stitch, pull your fabric taut from top to bottom. You may need to tie off and start a new thread; check that you are happy with the stretch before tying off. This process can be challenging as you constantly ensure you have not distorted your image. Trust the process; if you are not happy, it's easily reversible, and you can restart at any point.

Step 4

Once you are satisfied with the top-to-bottom stretch, repeat the process from left to right. Before doing this, carefully fold in your corners. Avoid cutting away any excess fabric in the corners, as this limits your ability to make changes if needed. Once you have stretched your fabric from top to bottom and left to right, you should have a beautifully stretched piece ready to frame.

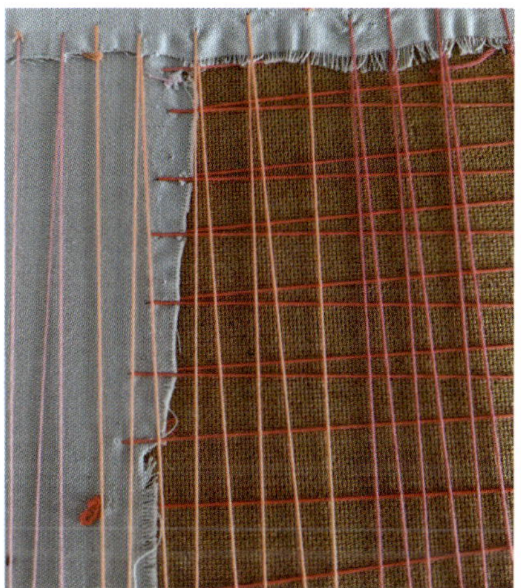

Stretched embroidery across hardboard.

Choosing a frame

When choosing a frame, try various thicknesses and colours to see what best showcases your work. You might want to highlight a specific colour in your piece by using it on the frame. Often, an understated frame will best complement your work and show it off to its full potential.

STRETCHING AND FRAMING A CANVAS

As I mentioned earlier in the book, you may choose to stretch your own canvases or buy them as your preferred method for embroidery. I have quite often incorporated paint with my pieces so the canvas over stretcher bars is a great fit for my work. The difference between a framed canvas and an unframed canvas is rather surprising. A floating frame on an embroidery canvas gives it a layer of quality and finishing which receives a level of respect from the audience that an unframed canvas lacks. It looks professional and can add stature and definition to your piece.

Selecting Stretcher Bars, Choosing Fabric and Stretching for Embroidery

Selecting Stretcher Bars
Stretcher bars are wooden bars used to stretch fabric tightly, creating a sturdy and even surface for embroidery. Here's how to select the right stretcher bars:

- Measure the size of your intended embroidery piece. Stretcher bars come in various lengths, giving you the freedom to choose something just right. Choose bars that are slightly larger than your fabric to ensure there is enough space to secure the fabric tightly.
- Consider the depth of the bars. Standard depth is usually around 2cm, but deeper bars, approximately 4cm, can provide extra support for larger pieces.
- Select high-quality, kiln-dried wood to prevent warping. Look for smooth, splinter-free surfaces to avoid snagging your fabric and ensure the bars have mitred (angled) corners for a perfect fit when assembled. Choose bars that fit together snugly and securely. Some bars come with interlocking joints that don't require additional tools or fasteners.

Choosing an Appropriate Fabric
Choosing the right fabric is crucial for a successful embroidery project. Here are key factors to consider:

Fabric type
- Linen: Durable and has a tight weave, making it ideal for detailed work.
- Cotton: Common and easy to work with, available in various weaves like Aida, which is popular for cross-stitch.
- Silk: Luxurious but delicate, suitable for fine and detailed embroidery.
- Evenweave: Great for projects requiring uniformity, such as counted thread work.

Fabric weight and weave
- Choose a medium to heavyweight fabric with a stable structure to withstand the tension of stretching and stitching. Ensure the weave is appropriate for your technique. For instance, Aida is perfect for cross-stitch due to its grid-like weave.
- Fabric size: Cut the fabric at least 10cm–15cm larger than the stretcher bars on all sides to allow room for stretching and securing.

Step 1
Assemble the stretcher bars into a square or rectangular frame, ensuring all corners are at right angles. Use a mallet or hammer if necessary to ensure a tight fit.

Step 2
Lay the fabric face down on a clean, flat surface and centre the stretcher bar frame on top of the fabric.

Step 3
Starting in the middle of one side, staple the fabric to the back of the stretcher bar, pulling it taut. Move to the opposite side, pulling the fabric tight and placing another staple in the centre. Repeat this process for the remaining two sides, ensuring the fabric remains evenly taut. Continue stapling towards the corners, alternating sides and pulling the fabric tight each time. Fold the corners neatly and secure them with additional staples. Avoid cutting into the corners to create less bulk, unless you have chosen a particularly thick fabric.

Step 4
Check for any wrinkles or loose areas and adjust the tension by re-stapling if necessary. Like when putting your fabric in a hoop, it should have a drum-like sound. When I have finished stretching, I like to spray the stretched canvas with water. I find that as it dries and shrinks back a little, it leaves the canvas really taut and gives you a great start for stitching.

SELECTING AND ATTACHING A FLOATING FRAME TO A STRETCHED CANVAS

A floating frame, also known as a floater frame, provides a modern, sleek look giving the illusion that your canvas is 'floating' within the frame. This is a beautiful finish for any pre-stretched or self-stretched canvases. Here's how to select and attach a floating frame to your stretched canvas, and then attach the fixings ready to hang.

Selecting a Floating Frame

Measure the dimensions of your stretched canvas (height, width and depth). Choose a floating frame that is slightly larger than your canvas in height and width to create the desired 'floating' effect. The frame's depth should match or slightly exceed the depth of your stretched canvas. Floating frames are available in various materials such as wood, metal and composite. Select a material and finish that complements your artwork.

Consider the style of your artwork and the decor of the space where it will be displayed.

Attaching a Floating Frame to a Stretched Canvas

You will need:
Floating frame
Stretched canvas
Offset clips or L-brackets
Screws
Screwdriver or drill
Tape measure
Spirit level
Soft cloth

Step 1
Lay the floating frame face down on a clean, flat surface covered with a soft cloth to protect it from scratches. Centre your stretched canvas within the frame. There should be an even gap between the canvas and the frame edges, creating the floating effect. Use a tape measure to ensure the gap is even on all sides.

Step 2
Once the canvas is centred, attach offset clips or L-brackets to secure it in place. Offset clips are designed to bridge the gap between the frame and the canvas stretcher bar.

Place an offset clip at each corner of the frame, securing it to the stretcher bar. If your canvas is large, you may need to add additional clips along the sides for extra support. Use a screwdriver or drill to attach the clips to the back of the frame and the stretcher bars. Be careful not to overtighten, which could damage the frame or canvas.

Step 3
Check that the canvas is still centred and the gap between the canvas and frame is even. Adjust the clips if necessary. Ensure the canvas is secure and does not shift within the frame.

Step 4
You will need:
D-rings
Picture wire
Screws
Screwdriver or drill
Pencil
Measuring tape
Attach D-rings: measure about one-third of the way down from the top of the frame on each side. Mark these points with a pencil. Attach D-rings at these marks using screws. Ensure they are securely fastened but not overtightened as they could potentially damage your frame.

Step 5
Cut a length of picture wire about 1.5 times the width of the frame. Thread the picture wire through one D-ring, leaving about 7cm–8cm of wire. Wrap the excess wire around itself to secure it. Stretch the wire across the back of the frame and thread it through the other D-ring. Pull the wire tight but leave some slack to allow the wire to hang comfortably on a hook. Secure the wire by wrapping the excess around itself. Double-check that the wire is secure and not frayed.

Step 6

Ensure the picture wire is securely attached and that the frame is ready to hang. Use a level to check the alignment of the D-rings if necessary. By following these steps, you can successfully select and attach a floating frame to your stretched canvas and prepare it for hanging, ensuring your artwork is beautifully presented and professionally displayed.

Cherries. Cotton thread on painted cotton canvas.

Lemons, cotton thread on cotton.

News
Scientists pinpoint how stress causes heart attacks
David

CHAPTER 9

EMBROIDERY ENCORE!

Embroidery is an art form that should be synonymous with joy, relaxation and self-expression. It's a craft that invites you to immerse yourself in the creative process, allowing the needle and thread to bring your visions to life. To truly enjoy embroidery it's essential to approach it with a sense of leisure and pleasure, rather than as a task to be hurriedly completed.

Embroider at Your Own Pace

One of the most crucial aspects of enjoying embroidery is to ensure that you are never rushed. This craft thrives on patience and attention to detail, qualities that are best nurtured in an unhurried environment. When you sit down to embroider, choose a time when you can dedicate your full attention to it, free from distractions and time constraints. Perhaps it's a quiet evening after a long day, or a lazy Sunday afternoon.

By giving yourself the gift of time, you create a space where creativity can flourish.

Watercolour flowers on paper ready to be embroidered. Push the boundaries by embroidering on different materials and introducing extra mediums with embroidery.

Embroidery is not a race; it's a journey. Each stitch is a step, and there is no need to hurry. The beauty of embroidery lies in its meditative rhythm. Allow yourself to savour the process. Watch how the thread weaves through the fabric, how colours blend and patterns emerge. This mindful engagement can turn embroidery into a soothing ritual, one that provides a welcome escape from the hustle and bustle of daily life.

A Slice of Apple; cotton thread on cotton.

Embroidery workspace.

The author at work stitching Lost Love.

Pamela portrait detail; cotton thread on cotton.

The Importance of Loving Your Subject Matter

For embroidery to be truly enjoyable, it should be a reflection of your passions and interests. Choose subject matter that excites and inspires you. Whether it's a delicate floral pattern, a whimsical animal design or an intricate geometric motif, let

Close-up of work in progress on Lost Love.

your heart guide your choices. When you embroider something you love, your enthusiasm will be evident in every stitch.

Consider what makes you happy and what you are passionate about. If you love nature, perhaps a series of botanical designs will bring you joy. If you are fond of abstract art, let your imagination run wild with vibrant freeform shapes and colours. The subject matter is your canvas for self-expression, so don't be afraid to experiment and try new things. The more personal the design, the more connected you will feel to the final piece.

Creating for Yourself vs Creating to Sell

Embroidery can be a deeply personal hobby, but it can also be a source of income if you choose to sell your creations. Whether you are embroidering for your own enjoyment or for others, the underlying principle should be the same: enjoy the process. Hopefully through this book you have learnt a wide range of techniques and applications for embroidery. If you design embroidery kits for others to enjoy stitching, embroider to express your opinion or document

A collection of small pop hoops.

observations through thread, these chapters would have equipped you with a springboard start on forging your own routes through your embroidery journey.

When creating for yourself, let your imagination and preferences take the lead. There are no rules or expectations, just the pure pleasure of creating something beautiful for your own satisfaction. This freedom can be incredibly liberating, allowing you to explore and grow as an artist.

If you decide to sell your embroidered works, it's important to maintain the same level of enjoyment and passion. Creating a market does introduce some additional considerations, such as customer preferences and current trends, but it should not diminish your love for the craft. Find a balance between what you love to create and what your customers might appreciate. Your passion will shine through in your work, making your pieces more attractive and unique.

Embroidery is more than just a creative outlet – it can be a form of therapy. The repetitive motion of stitching can be incredibly calming, helping to reduce stress and anxiety. The focus required for detailed work can serve as a mental escape, allowing you to momentarily forget your worries and lose yourself in the flow of creation.

Moreover, completing an embroidery project, no matter how small, can bring a sense of accomplishment and pride. This can be especially rewarding if you've created something that is meaningful to you or someone else. The act of creating something beautiful with your own hands is a powerful reminder of your abilities and creativity.

In the world of embroidery, there is no rush, no urgency. It is a space where time slows down, allowing you to immerse yourself fully in the joy of creating. By choosing a subject matter that excites you and embroidering at a pace that feels right, you can turn this craft into a pleasurable and fulfilling part of your life. Whether you are stitching for yourself or creating pieces to share with others, the key is to savour every moment of the process. Let embroidery be a delightful expression of your unique self, one stitch at a time. It's been a joy to share my knowledge and years of experience with you.

Blossom; close-up of French knots.

GLOSSARY

Appliqué: A decorative sewing technique where pieces of fabric are cut into shapes and stitched over a larger piece of fabric to create a design or pattern. You can use hand stitching or a sewing machine to attach the pieces.

Colour theory: The theory of how colours behave, how to use and mix colours.

Complementary: Placing colours, patterns and textures together to enhance and emphasise their qualities.

Composition: The way in which a visual is placed together. A composition involves considering the placement of images, objects and shapes to form an attractive visual.

Contrast: When opposing colours, textures and patterns are placed together.

Dissolvable fabric: Used for some embroidery projects where the embroidery is left without a backing. The fabric is dissolved in water, leaving just the threads once a design has been stitched.

Embellish: Adding decorative details to enhance and make something more attractive.

Freehand machine embroidery: Using the needle on a sewing machine to draw freely. This involves lowering the feet on the machine and using your hands to guide the fabric in order to create an image, as if you were drawing.

Mixed media: Using a variety of ways to create an image or design within one art piece, for example painting a design and then adding details such as beads, sequins and embroidery to enhance the piece.

Sample: Testing out an idea on a small scale that documents a technique, fabric or style idea.

Skein: A length of thread or yarn that has been coiled, wrapped or spooled loosely ready to use.

Stabiliser: A layer of fabric that is often glued or sewn to other fabric to keep it steady or stable. A great help on some fabrics before embroidering.

Texture: How something feels to touch. For example, the texture of a fabric may be soft, smooth or bobbly.

INDEX

First published in 2025 by
The Crowood Press Ltd
Ramsbury, Marlborough
Wiltshire SN8 2HR

enquiries@crowood.com
www.crowood.com

British Library Cataloguing-in-Publication Data
A catalogue record for this book is available from the British Library.

For product safety-related questions, contact:
productsafety@crowood.com

ISBN 978 0 7198 4516 1

Cover design by Sergey Tsvetkov
Typeset by Envisage IT
Printed and bound in India by Parksons Graphics

ACKNOWLEDGMENTS

First and foremost, I would like to extend my deepest gratitude to my husband, whose unwavering support and encouragement have been the cornerstone of this book. Your constant motivation and belief in my passion for embroidery have kept me inspired every step of the way. Thank you for your incredible patience and understanding, especially as our home is a constant sea of threads, needles and fabric. Your willingness to embrace the creative chaos has allowed me to fully immerse myself in this craft.

To my husband, for your love, laughter and enduring support – this book would not have been possible without you. Thank you for being my greatest champion and for always keeping me motivated. Thank you for cheering me on through every stitch.

Not to forget a big thank you to The Crowood Press for the opportunity to share my experience and love of embroidery to a new audience, along with their patience as I navigated my way through writing this book for you all to enjoy.